D1507431

AMERICAN CITIES

AMERICAN CITIES

CHARTWELL
BOOKS, INC.

CHARTWELL BOOKS, INC.
A Division of
BOOK SALES, INC.
114 Northfield Avenue
Edison, New Jersey 08837

ISBN-13: 978-0-7858-2245-5
ISBN-10: 0-7858-2245-3

Cataloging-in-Publication data is available from the Library of Congress

Printed and bound in China

Design: Tony Stocks Compendium

PAGE 1: *Panorama of Times Square.*
© L. Clarke/CORBIS

PAGE 2/3: *Skyscrapers towering above the Chicago River, July 1997.*
© Joseph Sohm; Visions of America/CORBIS

RIGHT: *The statue of Paul Revere by Paul Singleton Copley dwarfs the spire of the historic Old North Church. Both are highlights of the "Freedom Trail" in Boston, MA.*
© Joseph Sohm; ChromoSohm Inc./CORBIS

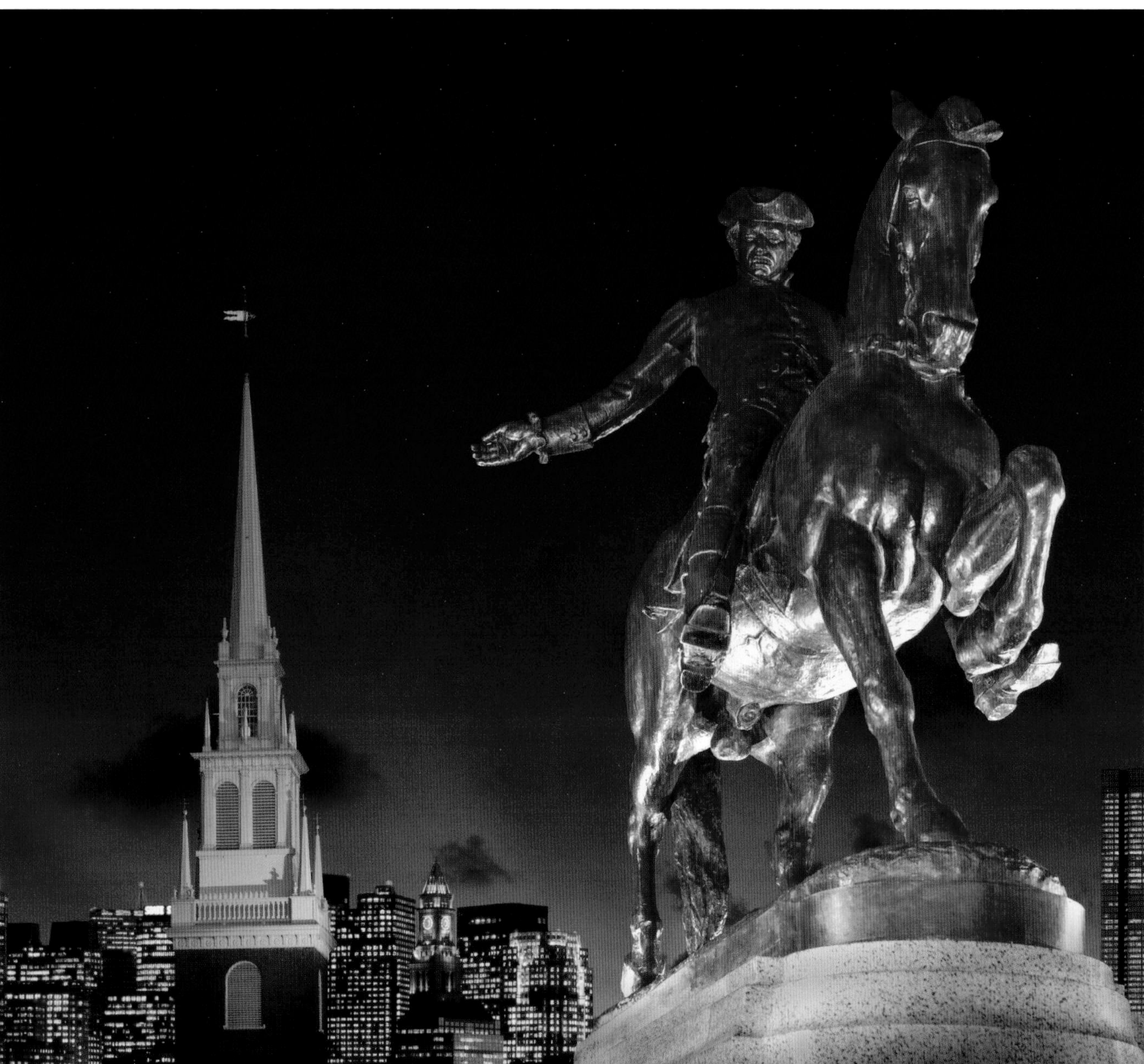

CONTENTS

INTRODUCTION

No country in the world can rival the United States for cultural diversity. And nowhere is that better reflected than in its major cities.

The names alone tell a fascinating story of their origins, betraying the nationality of their first settlers and, often, a clue as to those settlers' first impressions. Now, of course, those early pioneers would scarcely recognize the cities they founded all those years ago: natural disasters such as flood or fire, the Civil War of 1861–65, the development of new industry or an unexpected influx of people have all, in one way or another, played a part in shaping today's cities. Skylines have changed over time too, the high rise mixing with history, while the ethnic mix in the population that typifies the all-inclusive United States is often reflected in the architecture from region to region.

Transport systems, from the arrival of the railroads in the 19th century through motor transportation to air travel some years later, have also affected the way cities have developed as tourist or trade centers. Yet it was the natural waterways that existed long before the settlers arrived that proved the first links between cities, and many of the coastal areas first settled are major ports now. Water was also crucially important for cities that grew in desert regions, dams and irrigation helping turn arid waste into fields and vineyards that could support life and generate revenue.

In some cases, technology has superseded agriculture: computers have created a revenue-rich Silicon Valley. Other cities like Reno, Las Vegas, and Atlantic City have become meccas for gamblers, attracting them to areas where the tourist trade would otherwise be unlikely to take off and dazzling them with the prospect of riches. Talking of riches, the gold rushes of the 19th century were the making of some equally inhospitable areas: the major problem was accommodating the thousands of would-be citizens who appeared literally overnight to place a strain on existing infrastructure.

RIGHT: *Los Angeles skyline at night.*
© Pete Saloutos/CORBIS

ARCO
Sanwa Bank

Such bouts of prosperity ebb and flow, of course, and many a city has endured periods of hardship until a new transport link or industry revitalized it. The arrival of the automobile gave Cleveland and Detroit much-needed shots in the arm, for instance. Others, like Fresno, the proud "raisin-producing capital of the world," have merely capitalized on their good fortune in what nature has bestowed on them.

Cities are populated by people, and there is no doubt that some bear the imprint of major personalities to have lived, and sometimes died, in them: Martin Luther King in Atlanta and John F Kennedy in Dallas are two examples that had an impact on an international level. Yet the cultural importance of Berry Gordy's Motown record label on Detroit, or the hippie counterculture in San Francisco, both of which took off in the 1960s, was also felt on a global scale. Less happily, the Rodney King race riots and the cataclysmic events of 9/11 put Los Angeles and New York City into the headlines in 1992 and 2001 respectively.

The changing face of American cities reflects the development of a great nation. These pictures tell their own revealing story, and will fascinate readers of all ages.

RIGHT: *The Golden Gate Bridge was designed by Joseph Strauss and opened in 1937. At 4,200ft, it was the world's longest suspension bridge for 20 years. This is a January 1999 view.*
© Joseph Sohm; Visions of America/CORBIS

ALBUQUERQUE

Location 35.084°N 106.65°W
Area 180.6 square miles
Altitude 4,955 feet above sea level
City Population 448,607
Time Zone Mountain Daylight Saving

Albuquerque, the largest city in New Mexico, nestles in the Rio Grande valley below the majestic Sandia Mountains and is the seat of Bernalillo County. It is home to nearly one-third of the population of New Mexico but still manages to retain small-town qualities. Cultural influences from both Native Americans and early Hispanic settlers are still evident and give Albuquerque—incorporated in 1891—a unique character.

Although Spanish settlement began in the early 1600s, Native Americans rebelled against Spanish rule during the Pueblo Revolt of 1680 and the Spaniards abandoned the region. The area had long been settled by Native Americans who built large, multi-storied towns, called pueblos, some of which are still in existence today. Coronado, the Spanish explorer, stayed in the city while searching for the fabled seven cities of gold.

Modern-day Albuquerque was founded in 1706 and is named after the Duke of Alburquerque, then Viceroy of New Spain. Following the Mexican War of 1846–48, the city formally became part of the United States and was an important military post between 1846 and 1870. Confederate troops briefly held the city during the American Civil War, but a new settlement grew toward the end of the 19th century centered around the newly constructed railroad.

The city flourished as a farming community and center for health issues, which eventually enveloped the original Old Town in 1949. During the 1950s, growth was propelled by federal spending on nuclear research. Further development took place during the 1970s with the city's airport and convention center which were completed in the late 1980s.

Spanish colonial buildings, broad plazas and flat-roofed adobe houses can still be found in the old quarter of Albuquerque, along with the Church of San Felipe de Neri (1793), while modern buildings consist of lofty offices, hotels and fashionable shopping facilities. It is the seat of the University of New Mexico, founded in 1889, and features many museums and the fascinating Indian Pueblo Cultural Center.

RIGHT: *Restaurants along Central Avenue in Albuquerque. Twenty miles long, Central Avenue is the main artery of Albuquerque, part of Route 66.* © Richard Cummins/CORBIS

OVERLEAF: *In the heart of Albuquerque's Old Town is the Plaza, bordered by adobe buildings and the imposing church of San Felipe de Neri.* © Liz Hymans/CORBIS

Albuquerque and Sandia Crest—at 10,678ft the highest point of the Sandia mountains—from the observation deck at Sandia Peak. Reached by a 2.7-mile aerial tramway, the 15-minute ride takes you up towards the 10,000ft tops and a breath of cool air after a summer day. © Liz Hymans/CORBIS

ANAHEIM

Location 33.835°N 117.913°W
Area 48.9 square miles
Altitude 160 feet above sea level
City Population 328,014
Time Zone Pacific

Anaheim is best known for its tourist and convention industries, most notably, Disneyland and the Anaheim Convention Center. It is now an industrial center, making electronic and computer equipment, prepared foods, plastic products, fabricated metal products, consumer goods, motor vehicles, and molded rubber goods.

The nearby Santa Ana River and heim meaning "home" in German make up the name of Anaheim which was founded by German immigrants in 1857. Incorporated almost 20 years later, this settlement was designed as an experiment in communal living.

Once an orange grove, Anaheim is situated within Orange County in southwest California and sits within the southeast metropolitan area of Los Angeles. The early settlers produced wine, but the vines suffered extensively from disease in the late 1800s causing widespread damage. The area then became dominated by citrus nd walnut groves, but the city did not really develop or benefit from expansion until the opening of Disneyland during 1955.

The Walt Disney entertainment and media corporation based in Burbank, California was a leading name in family entertainment for much of the 20th century. The company unveiled the theme park at Anaheim in conjunction with the debut of *The Mickey Mouse Club* television series on ABC before going on to open other attractions in Walt Disney World, Orlando's Epcot Center, and Disneyland Paris.

The city underwent major redevelopment during the 1970s, with further extensive changes taking place in the downtown area during the 1990s. Anaheim is home to the California Angels (baseball) and the Anaheim Mighty Ducks (ice hockey).

Anaheim enjoys a Mediterranean climate and has a world-class business district, golf courses, theme parks, a stadium, and arenas. Ideally situated in close proximity to the ocean, mountains, lakes and deserts, it is easily accessible via airports, seaports, freeways and railways and enjoys a large and healthy local economy.

RIGHT: *Orange County and Anaheim are best known for Disneyland, the first theme park devoted to family entertainment. Disneyland now includes a second theme park, Disney's California Adventure (see page 16), and the Downtown Disney shopping and dining promenade seen here.*
© Robert Landau/CORBIS

FAR RIGHT: *Disneyland and the Anaheim Convention Center require a lot of hotel spaces: this is the swimming pool at the Hyatt.*
© Mark E. Gibson/CORBIS

Disney California Adventure—now three years old—is next to the original Disneyland and is themed on California's history. This photograph shows the Paradise Pier seaside amusement park with the California Screamin' roller coaster, Sun Wheel, 180ft Maliboomer vertical ride, and Orange Stinger.
© Macduff Everton/CORBIS

ANCHORAGE

Location 61.218°N 149.9°W
Area 1,697.2 square miles
Altitude 101 feet above sea level
City Population 260,283
Time Zone Alaskan

Anchorage, the largest city in Alaska, is a seaport on the arms of the Cook Inlet at the base of the Chugach Mountains. As a transport, commercial, and communications center, Anchorage takes advantage of natural resources such as petroleum, natural gas, and fishing and enjoys a healthy economy. This is further enhanced by the growing number of tourists visiting the area.

Native Americans and Russians have lived in Anchorage for more than 350 years. This is celebrated each year with the Anchorage Fur Rendezvous to remember trappers and miners who met annually in February and the Anchorage to Nome Iditarod Trail Sled Dog Race.

Although the community was established in 1915 as the construction headquarters of the Alaska Railroad, the city was not incorporated until 1920 when engineers of the U.S. Army started to lay out the city in a grid. This took a decade to complete, but Anchorage grew rapidly during World War II when it became the headquarters for the U.S. Alaska Defense Command. In 1942, the Alaska Highway was built to reinforce the defense of the West Coast and this connected the region to the rest of the country.

The Good Friday earthquake in March 1964 was the strongest ever recorded in North America and caused extensive damage which resulted in a number of deaths. Despite this, the city was quickly rebuilt and Anchorage experienced a boom in its economy during the late 1960s when oil was discovered in Prudhoe Bay. As a result of this find, the Alaska Pipeline was built during the mid-1970s.

As Anchorage is far south of the Arctic Circle it enjoys a surprisingly mild climate with temperatures reaching into the 20s Centigrade during the summer months. Protected by the Chugach Mountains and warmed by the Japanese currents of the Pacific Ocean, the climate remains mild all year round even though the winters bring snow. One major tourist attraction is the Portage Glacier, where large ice blocks can be seen falling off its face into the lake below.

RIGHT: *Pedestrians walk past Fourth Avenue Theater. Built in 1947, this Art Deco movie house seated over 1,000 in its opulent auditorium. Restored in the 1980s, it is now used for banquets and special functions.* © James Marshall/CORBIS

FAR RIGHT: *Anchorage homes covered with snow. Anchorage is located at a latitude of 61°N (about the same as Stockholm and St. Petersburg) so there's a lot of snow. The most populous city in Alaska, Anchorage holds nearly half the state's population.* © James Marshall/CORBIS

Anchorage is situated on a triangular peninsula bordered on the east by the Chugach Mountains, and on the northwest and southwest by the Cook Inlet, a large inlet of the Gulf of Alaska.
© Terry W. Eggers/CORBIS

ATLANTA

Location 33.748°N 84.388°W
Area 131.7 square miles
Altitude 1,050 feet above sea level
City Population 416,474
Time Zone Eastern

Situated on the eastern slopes of the Appalachian Mountains, Atlanta was founded during the 1830s as the southern terminal of the Western and Atlantic Railroad. This small location was aptly named Terminus and, as work progressed on the railroad, the settlement grew, changing its name to Marthasville in 1843. Atlanta was adopted in honor of the railroad in 1845, and the capital city of Georgia was incorporated two years later.

Fast-growing rail connections quickly established Atlanta as a commercial center and by the time of the American Civil War (1861–65), it had a population of more than 9,000. Atlanta became a vital Confederate stronghold during the war making it a prime target for Union General William T. Sherman who captured and razed much of the city in 1864. Despite this destruction, nearly 20,000 people had migrated to Atlanta by 1867.

The city experienced widespread racial tensions during the early 20th century including a 1906 race riot. The Ku Klux Klan and several anti-racial organizations established their headquarters there and racial segregation was rife until the end of World War II. Martin Luther King is probably Atlanta's most famous son and the National Historic Site encompasses both the church where he preached and the King Center where he is buried.

Atlanta hosted the 1996 Summer Olympics, but the occasion was marred when a bomb exploded in Centennial Olympic Park—the largest urban park built in the United States in the past 25 years. Although the area had become a popular tourist venue, there was only one fatality but more than 100 were injured. The Olympic Stadium has since been renamed Turner Field, and is home to the Atlanta Braves baseball team.

Atlanta enjoys rapid economic growth and is undoubtedly the business capital of the southeast. It is home to some of the largest companies in the United States including Coca-Cola, United Parcel Service, and the Delta airline.

RIGHT: *Atlanta skyline, looking west from the boulevard. SunTrust Plaza (One Peachtree Center)—seen at far right of this photograph—is 867ft high, the second tallest building in Atlanta. Center left is 191 Peachtree Tower, at 770ft Atlanta's fourth tallest; to the right of 191 Peachtree is the cylindrical Westin Peachtree Plaza which is 723ft tall. At far left is the Georgia Pacific Tower (697ft).*
© James Randklev/CORBIS

FAR RIGHT: *Giant baseballs line the street outside Turner Field, home of the Atlanta Braves, on July 26, 2004.*
© Scott Cunningham/Getty Images

35
Champions
'95 '97 '98 '99
'96
COMMISSIONER

A 1990s view of Atlanta showing (far right) Atlanta's tallest skyscraper, Bank of America Plaza, at 55 stories and 1,023ft the tallest building in the southern U.S.. Built in only 14 months and completed in 1992, much of the 90ft high spire is covered with gold leaf.
© Joseph Sohm; Visions of America/CORBIS

ATLANTIC CITY

Location 39.364°N 74.423°W
Area 11.3 square miles
Altitude 8 feet above sea level
City Population 40,517
Time Zone Eastern

Renowned for its rich cultural history, Atlantic City is often described as "the city built on sand" and is situated on the narrow Absecon Island on the Atlantic Ocean along the New Jersey coastline. The city's fortunes declined during the 1960s and 1970s, but economic growth was re-established after the legalization of gambling in 1978 and sparked a revival which is still in evidence with candy manufacturing and large gambling casinos the biggest industries today.

The beginning was rather different. In the early 1800s, Dr. Jonathan Pitney was one of the first settlers in an area with little more than sand, marshes, and wilderness. He saw the potential for investment and began inviting wealthy city dwellers to the coast to recuperate from the stresses of city living. The settlement became known as Absegami, meaning "little sea water." A proposed railroad to this obscure place fascinated investors and final plans for the railroad were decided in 1853. An eastern terminus was built and the city became incorporated in 1854. Grand hotels began to spring up and Atlantic City, as it had been unanimously named, became a major beach resort.

In 1870, a railroad conductor and a disgruntled hotel owner petitioned the city council asking that a mile-long walkway be established to keep the sand from reaching the beachfront hotels and railroad passenger cars. The result was the Atlantic City Boardwalk, the most famous walkway on the East Coast. At first, no commercial activities were allowed within 30 feet of the Boardwalk but, by 1883, almost 100 commercial sites had Boardwalk addresses. In 1916, after several storms and a hurricane, the final Boardwalk was built and is now the city's most romantic attraction.

Margaret Gorman, aged 15, became the first Miss America in Atlantic City in September 1921 when King Neptune crowned her in a publicity stunt in order to extend the summer season. The Miss America pageant has since become synonymous with Atlantic City.

RIGHT: *The Borgata Hotel, Casino, and Spa in Atlantic City. A joint venture between Boyd Gaming and MGM Mirage that opened in July 2003, the hotel has over 2,000 guest rooms and suites, 125,000 square feet of gaming, 145 gaming tables, 3,650 slot machines, as well as restaurants, boutiques, a 50,000 square foot spa, and parking for over 7,000 cars.* © Bob Krist/CORBIS

FAR RIGHT: *The Atlantic City boardwalk—the nation's first—and waterfront casinos. There are 13 in total: the Atlantic City Hilton, Bally's Park Place and Wild West Casino, the Borgata, Caesar's, the Claridge, Harrah's, Resorts, Sands, Showboat, Tropicana, Trump Marina, Trump Plaza (illustrated here), and the Trump Taj Mahal.* © Bill Ross/CORBIS

ALL STA
CASINO

The Taj Mahal casino sits on a 20-acre site. It was built by Donald Trump at the north end of the Boardwalk and opened on April 2, 1990. It is connected to Resorts and Showboat (at right) via a skywalk. © Richard Berenholtz/CORBIS

AUSTIN

Location 30.266°N 97.742°W
Area 251.5 square miles
Altitude 501 feet above sea level
City Population 656,562
Time Zone Central

Located in the center of the Lone Star State, Austin is the seat of Travis County. The city lies on the Colorado River near the Balcones Escarpment and is the base for numerous manufacturing and commercial operations while offering extensive leisure and educational facilities.

Franciscan missionaries established temporary missions in the area during 1730, choosing sites traditionally occupied by the Native American inhabitants. A community named Waterloo was settled in 1838 on the north bank of the river and a year later was chosen as the capital of the Republic of Texas, a status confirmed by an 1850 state election. The city was incorporated in 1839 and its name changed to Austin in honour of Stephen F. Austin, the man considered the "father" of Texas.

During the Civil War, Austin became a site for Confederate army facilities and volunteers organized a light infantry company. In 1871, the Houston and Texas Central Railroad arrived and industrialization soon began with the construction of a dam and power plant on the river. The dam had to be rebuilt in 1912 following flood damage, a constant problem until the 1930s when the Colorado River Authority constructed a series of dams and reservoirs known locally as the Highland Lakes.

For much of its history, Austin's economy was dominated by the state and federal government as well as the University of Texas. During the 1980s the city became popular with computer technology organizations which helped diversify the economy. Austin is renowned for being the "Live Music Capital of the West," having become popular with country and roots musicians. The city's annual SXSW (South by Southwest) festival is now a major event on the music-business calendar.

Austin welcomes the largest colony of bats in North America when, from April to September, the Congress Avenue Bridge is home to more than one million Mexican free-tailed bats. Other attractions include Barton Springs, a spring-fed swimming area that maintains a constant 20°C (68°F) temperature.

RIGHT: *The University of Texas Tower was built in the Spanish Revival style in 1936. It is 307ft high, has a 56-bell carillon, the largest and tallest carillon in Texas. The largest bell weighs in at 7,350lb. However, it is unfortunately best known for the events of August 1, 1966, when Charles Joseph Whitman shot and killed 13 people, hitting 30 others, from the observation deck.*
© CORBIS

FAR RIGHT: *The Budweiser Clydesdales lead a parade of bikers down Congress Avenue May 30, 2003. The three-day Republic of Texas Biker Rally ran through June 1.*
© Matt Archer/Getty Images

Panorama of Austin, looking northeast from Riverside Park on the banks of the Colorado River. At right, in the foreground, is the Congress Avenue Bridge and, past it, the San Jacinto Center (310ft), clad in Texas creme limestone and Llano rose granite. At left 100 Congress rises to 320ft; in the center is One Congress Plaza (391ft). The photograph doesn't show Austin's tallest building, which since 2004 has been the 515ft Frost Bank Tower. © D. Boone/CORBIS

BALTIMORE

Location 39.290°N 76.612°W
Area 80.8 square miles
Altitude 100 feet above sea level
City Population 651,154
Time Zone Eastern

An independent city in northern Maryland, Baltimore sits near the head of the Patapsco River on Chesapeake Bay. It is one of the busiest ports in the United States—boasting one of the world's largest natural harbors—and a major industrial, research and educational center.

Originally settled by Native Americans known as Susquehannock, Europeans began exploring the area in the early 1600s but settlement did not begin in earnest until 1661. From humble beginnings as a tobacco port in 1729, the town rapidly flourished as a flour-milling and shipbuilding center that benefited from trade with Europe and the Caribbean. It was named in honor of the British founders of the Maryland Colony, known as the Barons of Baltimore.

Baltimore has several claims to fame: as home to Congress during the American Revolution because of the British occupation of Philadelphia and as the inspiration behind *The Star-Spangled Banner*, written by American lawyer and poet Francis Scott Key after an 1814 battle around Fort McHenry. It was home to writer Edgar Allan Poe and the birthplace of legendary baseball player Babe Ruth.

Following the construction of the Baltimore and Ohio Railroad, the Sparrows Point steel mill was opened and led to further heavy industrial development. Both world wars promoted industrial growth—particularly in steel and oil refining—while 1960s redevelopment helped revitalize the Downtown and Inner Harbor areas.

Today, Baltimore's economy focuses on research and development, especially in aquaculture, pharmaceuticals, and medical supplies and services; the city is home to more than 60 federal research laboratories as well as private ventures. Baltimore also boasts the Columbus Center and a large marine biotechnology center opened in 1994.

The first Catholic Church ever built in the United States was the Basilica of the Assumption of the Blessed Virgin Mary, and there are also monuments dedicated to Christopher Columbus and George Washington. The Lacrosse Hall of Fame Museum at John Hopkins University celebrates the game created by Native Americans and still played today.

RIGHT: *Baltimore is a characterful city with many historic areas, although much of downtown was destroyed by fire in 1904. These brick row houses are on Charles Street in Mount Vernon District.*
© Paul A. Souders/CORBIS

ABOVE: *Aerial view of the campus of Johns Hopkins University. The white tower is atop Gilman Hall, designed by Douglas Thomas of Parker, Thomas, and Rice, the firm won the 1904 competition for an overall campus design. Gilman Hall was named for Daniel Coit Gilman, the first president of the university, and began the tradition of Georgian buildings on campus. Construction began in 1913, and the building was dedicated on May 21, 1915.*
© Richard T. Nowitz/CORBIS

OVERLEAF: *A gleaming light in urban regeneration, Baltimore's Inner Harbor was completely rebuilt at the end of the last century. Two of Baltimore's main attractions are on the harbor: the National Aquarium and the USS* Constellation, *the U.S. Navy's first ship. The Inner Harbor skyline shows off: at left, Baltimore's tallest building, the Legg Mason Building (529ft, designed by Vlastimil Koubek); next (illuminated) the Bank of America Building (509ft); then 100 East Pratt Street (418ft); the building with the dark roof is Commerce Place (454ft); and at right, the World Trade Center (405ft) was designed by I. M. Pei.*© Richard T. Nowitz/CORBIS

LEGG
MASON

BATON ROUGE

Location 30.450°N 91.154°W
Area 76.8 square miles
Altitude 53 feet above sea level
City Population 227,818
Time Zone Central

Baton Rouge, the capital of Louisiana, is situated at the head of deep water on the Mississippi River and has facilities for handling both ocean-going vessels and river barges.

The region was long inhabited by Native Americans of the Houma and Bayou Goula tribes but was settled in 1719 by the French who built a fort there to protect travelers venturing north from New Orleans. The city's name, the French for "red stick," is said to commemorate a cypress tree of that color that marked the boundaries between the hunting grounds of the two tribes.

In 1763, Baton Rouge came under British control, but passed to the Spanish during the American Revolution. France reacquired the area in 1800, but when the French sold most of present-day Louisiana to the United States in 1803, the Spanish claimed it back as part of West Florida. Residents rebelled against Spanish rule in 1810 and, as a result, the independent West Florida Republic was established which became a territory of the United States.

Baton Rouge was incorporated as a city in 1817, becoming the capital of Louisiana in 1849. During the Civil War, Louisiana joined the Confederacy, but Baton Rouge was captured by Union forces in 1862 and remained under their control until the end of the war in 1865.

Protected on the highlands above the Mississippi River, the city's location encouraged industrial development and a first refinery was built in 1909 which led to Baton Rouge becoming synonymous with refining and petrochemical production.

Baton Rouge today remains one of the leading centers for major petrochemicals manufacturing and is also an important distribution point for the large quantities of soya beans and sugarcane produced in the surrounding areas.

RIGHT: *Sitting in 50 acres of gardens, the Art Deco Louisiana State Capitol Building was ordered by Huey Long—the "Kingfish"—in 1931. He died in the building in 1935, assassinated by a local doctor.* © D. Boone/CORBIS

OVERLEAF, LEFT: *An aerial view of Baton Rouge from the 1980s, showing that Long's decree keeping his 27-story Capitol tower the tallest point in the city had been honored.* © Michael Busselle/CORBIS

OVERLEAF, RIGHT: *From 1850 until 1931 this was the Louisiana state capitol; now it is the Old State Capitol Center for Political and Governmental History.* © Danny Lehman/CORBIS

The Mississippi at Baton Rouge is known for its paddle-wheel tourist and gaming boats. This is one of the landing stages.
© Richard Cummins/CORBIS

BOISE

Location 43.613°N 116.202°W
Area 63.8 square miles
Altitude 2,730 feet above sea level
City Population 185,787
Time Zone Mountain Daylight Saving

Located on the river of the same name in the southwest of Idaho, Boise is home to the headquarters of several major corporations including manufacturers of computer microchips, processed foods, and forest products, as well as construction and service companies. It is the economic center for much of Idaho's metropolitan region and boasts the National Interagency Fire Center which co-ordinates fighting wild fires throughout the United States.

Shoshone Native Americans thwarted the efforts of French-Canadian fur trappers to settle the region in the early part of the 19th century. The name of the city is derived from the French *boisé* meaning wooded which was how the French-Canadian trappers referred to the tree-lined Boise River.

Permanent settlement was not achieved until 1863 following the discovery of gold in the area. The site for the city of Boise was selected next to Fort Boise, a U.S. military base. Located at the crossroads of the Oregon Trail and routes to the gold mines, the city enjoyed rapid growth. By 1870, the number of Chinese immigrants that had come to mine gold near Boise outnumbered the white miners who later became farmers, merchants and restaurateurs in the area.

Boise was incorporated as a city in 1864 and was elected at the same time to become the capital of Idaho Territory. Boise remained the seat of government for the State of Idaho when statehood was granted in 1890.

The National Reclamation Act of 1902 provided for the construction of the Arrowrock Dam which allowed for expansion in irrigated farming, thereby aiding the city's expansion. Further development took place after 1925 when the main line of the Union Pacific Railroad passed through the city. Substantial growth was not experienced, however, until the mid-1980s when two major electronics manufacturing plants were established and Boise remains a high-tech city today.

RIGHT AND FAR RIGHT: *The Idaho State Capitol on Jefferson and Capitol Boulevard was built in 1905 to resemble the capitol building in Washington D.C. It took 15 years to complete and it is the only state capitol heated by a geothermal well.* © Joseph Sohm; ChromoSohm Inc./CORBIS and Kevin R. Morris/CORBIS

PIZZA
HUT
RAMADA
INN
Ann Morrison
Park

Left: *Snow cloaks the hills above the Capitol Building and Boise's bustling streets.* © Macduff Everton/CORBIS

Right: *House with sleds.* © Michael S. Lewis/CORBIS

BOSTON

Location 42.358°N 71.06°W
Area 48.4 square miles
Altitude 20 feet above sea level
City Population 589,141
Time Zone Eastern

Boston's many fans would claim the city represents the ideal combination of history and progress. Its skyline reflects the equal weight of tradition and modernity, landmarks like the Customs House clock tower and Old North Church vying with the Government Center.

Boston was founded in 1630 by the Puritans, and played a major part in the historic struggle for independence from the British. Indeed the famed 'Tea Party' of 1773, when colonists disguising themselves as native American Indians dumped several hundred chests of tea from the decks of British vessels, took place in the selfsame deep water harbor that has brought the city so much of its prosperity.

George Washington took charge of the American response after British troops occupied the city, and it was the events of 1775 and 1776, from Paul Revere's "midnight ride" to the eventual defeat of the British, that secured Boston its cherished status as the "Cradle of Independence." Prosperity earned it another title, the "Athens of America," and soon many thousands of European immigrants would arrive keen to share in the city's riches. The city also increased hugely in size in the late 1800s when the neighboring towns of Roxbury, West Roxbury, Dorchester, Charlestown, Brighton, and Hyde Park were incorporated.

But decline was soon to follow as the city was undercut by the cheaper workforce of the southern states, and it wasn't until the mid-20th century that the pendulum began to swing back, boosted by the educational establishments of Harvard and MIT attracting some of the nation's brightest minds. Indeed, the current skyline bears the mark of MIT alumnus I.M. Pei, who designed numerous government skyscrapers and office blocks. However, Boston cherishes its past, and among the historical monuments open to the public are Paul Revere's 17th-century house, the Old South Meetinghouse where patriots gathered during the Revolution and the Boston Light which, dating from 1716, is claimed to be the oldest lighthouse in the United States.

RIGHT: *Boston Common and Downtown Boston seen from the John Hancock Tower. Set aside as common land in 1634, the Boston Common was on the sea shore for 200 years, grazed by cattle.*
© Bill Ross/CORBIS

RIGHT: *Historic Park Street Church was built in 1809 and during the War of 1812 the basement was used for storing gunpowder—hence the nickname "Brimstone Corner." The abolitionist William Lloyd Garrison gave his first anti-slavery speech from the pulpit here.* © Robert Holmes/CORBIS

Downtown Boston seen from across the Charles River in Cambridge: centre left is One Boston Place, at 601ft Boston's fourth tallest building; the Federal Reserve Bank Building (second from right) at 614ft is the third, and One Financial Center (far right, 590ft) the seventh. The tallest buildings in Boston—the John Hancock Tower (790ft) and the Prudential Tower (750ft)—are in the Back Bay/Beacon Hill neighborhood. © Joseph Sohm; Visions of America/CORBIS

INSET: *Historic Faneuil Hall is awash in Christmas lights. It was built in 1742 for the merchant Peter Faneuil, a French Huguenot who gave the hall to the town for use as its central meeting and marketplace. The original building was destroyed in 1761 by fire but was quickly reconstructed.* © Darren McCollester/Newsmakers/Getty Images

BUTTE

Location 46.003°N 112.533°W
Area 40.3 square miles
Altitude 92 feet above sea level
City Population 33,336
Time Zone Mountain Daylight Saving

Pronounced "Byoot," the seat of Silver Bow county in southwest Montana was established in 1862 and incorporated some 17 years later. A fire in 1879 burned down the business district, causing the city council to decree that all new buildings there be built from brick or stone—most still stand today and make Butte a city that fascinates historians.

Mining was Butte's sole raison d'etre and the lynchpin of its economy from the very beginning, and an impressive selection of minerals, including zinc, silver, manganese, gold, lead, molybdenum, and arsenic have been found in the region.

But it is copper, discovered around 1880, that put the city on the map: it is estimated that Butte supplied around one third of the copper for the United States in the late 1800s and the early 1900s, when the majority of the pits were owned by the Anaconda Mining Company. Cost-cutting eventually led to the adoption of strip mining where entire hillsides were removed. The Berkeley, a huge open-pit mine, was opened in 1955, with controversial results after some 20 percent of Butte's population was forced to relocate due to its operations. The pit was abandoned in 1982, by which time few of the city's inhabitants worked in mining.

Discarded heavy metals have entered the ecological system over the years, to the extent that the local river—the Clark Fork River—was sometimes seen to run red. The city is now the largest "Superfund" site in the U.S., such has been mining's negative effect on the environment. A number of pollution control companies are now based there.

More positively, Butte is the headquarters of Deerlodge National Forest. Local attractions include many mining and mineral museums, Our Lady of the Rockies, and the Copper King Mansion, once the home of U.S. senator and copper magnate William A. Clark who, with Anaconda's Marcus Daly, contested the title of "King Copper."

RIGHT: *Our Lady of the Rockies—a 90ft statue of Mary, the mother of Jesus—overlooks Butte, Montana. Located on the Continental Divide, a helicopter put the statue in place 3,500ft above the city.* © Jan Butchofsky-Houser/CORBIS

FAR RIGHT: *Butte was once the major copper mining center of the world and one of the largest cities in the west during the 1900s. Up the hill—the "Richest Hill on Earth"—lies old Butte.* © Jan Butchofsky-Houser/CORBIS

SALOON
UNION HALL

FAR LEFT: *Today Butte's mining past is reflected in its Museum of Mining on the site of Orphan Girl Mine and Hell Roarin' Gulch, an authentic reproduction of an 1890s' mining camp.* © Michael S. Lewis/CORBIS

LEFT: *A detail view of one of the 4,000 historic buildings in Downtown Butte. This city contains one of the largest National Historic Landmark Districts in the United States. These include some of the country's first tall buildings, elegant mansions, vintage Victorian homes, boarding houses and hotels, and miners' cottages that provided shelter for an estimated 100,000 people.* © Dave G. Houser/CORBIS

CHARLESTON

Location 32.776°N 79.931°W
Area 97.0 square miles
Altitude 118 feet above sea level
City Population 96,650
Time Zone Eastern

Situated between the Ashley and Cooper rivers on a narrow peninsula in southeast Carolina, Charleston heads a broad bay leading to the Atlantic Ocean. This strategic position has enabled it to develop as a major port in the southeast of the U.S. and allows both ocean vessels and coastal trade to take advantage of the city. The United States Navy and Army have both occupied sites to the north of the city.

Founded in 1670 on the west bank of the Ashley River at Albemarle Point, Charleston was originally named after King Charles II of England. However, the settlement was moved to its present site some ten years later and the new community prospered as a distribution hub for the region's rice, indigo and cotton plantations. It was also synonymous for being the biggest port in the United States to be involved in the burgeoning slave trade.

During the mid-18th century, the settlement became well known as a cultural center, with a diverse population including French Huguenots and the largest Jewish community in the American colonies.

Two British naval attacks in 1776 and 1779 were successfully overcome during the American Revolution, but Charleston was finally captured in 1780 and remained occupied for another two years. The city, whose name was then shortened from the original Charles Town, was incorporated in 1783 and endured the loss of state capital status seven years later when this honor was bestowed upon Columbia.

It was at Fort Sumter, one of three forts at the mouth of the harbor, that the American Civil War began on April 12, 1861. Industrial wealth followed the end of hostilities when phosphates were discovered in 1867, and prosperity was furthered by the establishment of a naval shipyard and other employers with military connections during the two world wars.

Charleston is no stranger to the forces of Mother Nature. A major earthquake caused major damage to the city in 1886, while Hurricane Hugo battered the city just over a century later.

RIGHT: *Charleston is an elegant city on the tip of a peninsula between the Cooper and Ashley rivers. It boasts over 1,500 historic buildings—in spite of fire in 1861, the advent of Union troops in 1865, an earthquake in 1886 and various hurricanes, the worst being Hugo in 1989.* © David Butow/Corbis

ABOVE RIGHT: *The South Carolina Society Hall, built in 1804, stands on Charleston's Meeting Street. It was designed by Gabriel Manigault, a gentleman architect who introduced the Adamesque style to the city after studying in Europe.* © Bob Krist/CORBIS

CHARLESTON · SOUTH CAROLINA
FULTON LANE
INN
202

Porches, palms, and mansions on South Battery Street seen from the boardwalk—elegant, historic Charleston at its most beautiful. © Joseph Sohm; ChromoSohm Inc./CORBIS

CHARLOTTE

Location 35.226°N 80.843°W
Area 242.3 square miles
Altitude 850 feet above sea level
City Population 540,828
Time Zone Eastern Standard Time

Charlotte, the largest city in the state of North Carolina, is located in the region of Piedmont Plateau near the Catawba River and is the seat of Mecklenburg County. The city lies at the heart of a thriving metropolis that incorporates seven counties and even extends into South Carolina. It is one of the principal banking centers of the United States, while other major industries include printing, chemical manufacture, processed food, micro-electronics, textiles, furniture, machinery, metal, and paper products, all of which are important for the city's economy.

German, Scottish, and Irish immigrants settled the region in the mid-18th century and the city, named after Charlotte Sophia of Mecklenburg-Strelitz, wife of King George III of England, was incorporated in 1768.

Created to oppose British rule, the Mecklenburg Declaration of Independence was said to have been signed in Charlotte by residents of Mecklenburg County on May 20, 1775, over a year before the Declaration of Independence was issued. During the American Revolution, British General Charles Cornwallis occupied the town, describing Charlotte as "a hornet's nest of rebellion."

Gold was discovered in the area in 1799 and though the city grew rapidly, prosperity was further increased with the development of the textile industry and the arrival of the railroad. During the Civil War, President of the Confederacy Jefferson Davis convened his cabinet at Charlotte for the last time in April 1865.

Of interest is the Mint Museum of Art, which is housed in a reconstructed former building of the United States Mint, the Charlotte Museum of History and the former home (and oldest surviving residence of Mecklenburg County) of Hezekiah Alexander, writer of the first constitution of North Carolina. Charlotte is also home to the Charlotte Hornets (basketball) and the Carolina Panthers (football) teams.

LEFT: *An evening view of the Charlotte skyline dominated by the 871ft Bank of America Corporate Center, designed by Cesar Pelli. At night the top looks like a crown that Charlotte's namesake, Queen Charlotte, wife of George III of Britain, could have worn. The building has 60 floors—one, it is said, for each year of her reign. To the right in this photograph is the Hearst Tower* *(see page 60).*

LEFT: *The Hearst Tower was opened on November 14, 2002, is 659ft tall, and has 47 floors—32 of which are in the tower, 15 in the podium below.* © Richard Cummins/CORBIS

BELOW: *U.S. Air Force fighter jets make a flyover prior to the start of the NASCAR Coca-Cola 600 at Lowe's Motor Speedway. The Coca-Cola 600 was started by NASCAR to stage a Memorial Day weekend event that would rival the Indy 500 and is the longest regularly scheduled motor race conducted over an oval circuit anywhere in the world.* © Doug Pensinger/Getty Images

FAR RIGHT: *Linebacker Brian Allen (#52), defensive tackle Omari Jordan (#91), and defensive end Al Wallace (#96) lead the Carolina Panthers onto the field during player introductions before the game against the Green Bay Packers at Bank of America Stadium on September 13, 2004. The Packers won 24–14. In 1993 Jerry Richardson was awarded the first new NFL franchise since 1976. Two years later Carolina and fellow expansion team Jacksonville Jaguars began to play. Two years later, in 1996, the team qualified for the playoffs; by 2004 they had reached the Superbowl where they lost a close-fought game to the Patriots by a field goal in the dying seconds.* © Craig Jones/Getty Images

RIGHT: *Another Charlotte expansion team. Here a performer jumps over children during a street party for the unveiling of the Charlotte Bobcats expansion NBA team on June 11, 2003.* © Kent Smith/NBAE via Getty Images

CHICAGO

Location 41.85°N 87.65°W
Area 5,618 square miles
Altitude 583 feet above sea level
City Population 2,896,016
Time Zone Central

Chicago is justly famous for its leading role in the development of modern architecture, most notably through the work of such luminaries as Louis Sullivan and Frank Lloyd Wright. The first Europeans to discover the Chicago area were Father Jacques Marquette, a French-born Jesuit missionary and Louis Jolliet, a Canadian explorer in 1673.

The Chicago area was then traveled by traders and explorers for some years but little is known about it until around 1779 when the pioneer settler Jean Baptiste Point du Sable, an African-American from Sainte-Domingue (Haiti), built the first permanent settlement at the mouth of the river just east of the present Michigan Avenue Bridge on the north bank. In 1795 a treaty between the federal government and the Native Americans saw a tract of land at the mouth of the Chicago River ceded to the United States. This was the site of the future city of Chicago. In 1803 the War Department ordered the construction of a fort at the mouth of the river. Within a year Fort Dearborn, named in honor of the Secretary of War, was completed. For some years the garrison was peaceful and trade flourished. However, the outbreak of the War of 1812 with Great Britain moved the government to order the evacuation of the fort. The threatening attitude of the Indians led the entire population of the settlement to follow the garrison. After leaving the fort, the evacuees were attacked by Indians and many of the party were massacred and the fort was destroyed. In 1816 the fort was rebuilt and was thereafter occupied by United States troops for 21 years.

Chicago was under the jurisdiction of Indiana Territory and Illinois Territory from 1801 to 1818. Then, in 1818, Illinois was admitted to statehood, and Chicago was placed successively under the counties of Crawford, Clark, Pike, Fulton, Putnam attached to Peoria, and in 1831, Cook County.

On August 12, 1833, the Town of Chicago was incorporated with a population of 350. The first boundaries of the new town were Kinzie, Desplaines, Madison, and State streets, which included an area of about three-eighths of a square mile. The name Chicago derived from the Indians but it is not known which tribe named the town. One generally accepted view is that the name comes from the Indian words for either wild onion or skunk, but some historians believe that the word Chicago denoted strong or great.

RIGHT: *The Chicago skyline at sunrise—the huge bulk of the Hancock Center, with its distinctive X-bracing, looms out of the gloom. Constructed in 1969, it is 1,136ft high, has 100 floors, and was designed by architects Skidmore, Owings & Merrill.* © Joseph Sohm; ChromoSohm Inc./CORBIS

FAR RIGHT: *Runners move past Marina Towers on State Street during the LaSalle Bank Chicago Marathon October 12, 2003. The two towers are 588ft high with 61 floors and were the tallest reinforced concrete buildings in the world until surpassed by 1000 Lake Shore Plaza.* © Jonathan Daniel/Getty Images

BELOW: *Two women read a cow locations map as they visit the "Cows On Parade" Art Exhibition in Chicago.* © John Zich/Getty Images

An aerial view of Chicago shows Lincoln Park in the foreground and Diversey Harbor and Lake Michigan at left. The John Hancock Center is the tall building at left center; to its right is Chicago's second tallest, the Aon Center (1,136ft) originally called "Big Stan" as it was the Standard Oil Building; the tall building at right is Chicago's tallest, the Sears Tower. The world's tallest building until Petronas Towers in Kuala Lumpar, Malaysia, was completed, the Sears Tower stands 1,450ft tall, has 108 floors and was constructed in 1974. Like the Hancock Center it was designed by the firm of Skidmore, Owings & Merrill, who have designed over 450 buildings including the enormous Russia Tower planned to rise to 2,126ft over Moscow. © Joseph Sohm; ChromoSohm Inc./CORBIS

LEFT: *Hundreds of musicians display their tubas after completing Tuba Christmas December 18, 2003. Over 400 tuba players participated in the annual holiday event playing Christmas carol favorites.* © Getty Images

FAR LEFT: *Chicago at twilight: Sears is at right and the Aon Center at left.* © Randy Faris/CORBIS

CINCINNATI

Location 39.161°N 84.456°W
Area 78.0 square miles
Altitude 683 feet above sea level
City Population 331,285
Time Zone Eastern

Situated strategically on the north bank of the Ohio River, Cincinnati was a focal point for those migrating west during the 19th century and hence was dubbed "The Gateway to the West." The third largest city in Ohio, it is the seat of Hamilton County and acts as a major transport, industrial, commercial and cultural center for the region.

One of the first permanent European settlements in Ohio since the late 18th century after settlers were attracted when the army built Fort Washington, the city was named in honor of the Society of Cincinnati, an association of officers in the American Revolution. This was itself named after Roman statesman Lucius Quinctius Cincinnatus.

Incorporated in 1819, the city became a major center for north–south commerce, both by land and by river. The Ohio River was a principal route connecting the east with the nation's growing frontier and was of paramount importance with the arrival of steamboat travel in 1811.

Cincinnati's ties to the south provoked mixed reactions during the Civil War and the city became a center of activity by the Copperheads (those opposed to fighting the war). The underground railroad, an informal system for moving slaves from the oppressive south to freedom in the north, passed through Cincinnati but trade was disrupted by hostilities and traffic began to bypass the city as new railroads allowed Chicago to become the region's principal crossroads. Cincinnati's economy suffered greatly but was slowly revived by the introduction of a railroad to Chattanooga, Tennessee, serving the south.

William Howard Taft, a member of a prominent local family holding several federal political positions, was born in the city and spent his early childhood there before going on to become the 27th U.S. President.

Urban renewal and redevelopment began during the mid-1960s and 1970s, designed to revitalize businesses and the riverfront district. The city has a heritage that includes those from many immigrant backgrounds, particularly Germans, Jews, ethnic minorities, and the Irish.

RIGHT: *The Great American Ballpark and Downtown Cincinnati from the other side of the Ohio River. This structure was built alongside and replaced Cinergy Field (see page 70) which was destroyed on December 29, 2002. The suspension bridge in the foreground is the Roebling Suspension Bridge erected in 1866. Originally called the Covington and Cincinnati Bridge, it was renamed after its designer, John A. Roebling.* © Jerry Driendl/Getty Images

INSET: *This view of Cincinnati's skyscrapers shows (at center left) the city's tallest building, the Carew Tower. It is 574ft tall and was constructed in 1931. Next to it, the white PNC Tower (495ft) was built in 1913 and designed by Garber & Woodward with Cass Gilbert as associate architect. When completed it was the fifth tallest building in the world. The Scripps Center (center right) was built in 1990 and is the city's third tallest building at 468ft. At far right the Atrium Towers complex was built in 1981–84 to designs by Skidmore, Owings & Merrill.* © W. Cody/CORBIS

STAR BANK
PROVIDENT

This early 1990s photograph shows the now-demolished Cinergy Field, the Roebling Suspension Bridge in the foreground, and two other important Cincinnati bridges: first, the Taylor-Southgate bridge which opened in 1995 in the exact location of the old Central Bridge carrying U.S. 27—the Dixie Highway—and behind it the graceful spans of the Daniel Carter Beard Bridge which opened to limited traffic in summer 1976 carrying I-471. Most know it as the Big Mac bridge. © Joseph Sohm; Visions of America/CORBIS

INSET: *April 1, 2002: thousands lined the streets of Downtown Cincinnati to watch the fire department roll down the street during the annual Opening Day Parade prior to the game at Cinergy Field between the Cincinnati Reds and the Chicago Cubs. The Reds won 5–4.* © Mark Lyons/Getty Images

CLEVELAND

Location 41.499°N 81.695°W
Area 77.6 square miles
Altitude 690 feet above sea level
City Population 478,403
Time Zone Eastern

Cleveland was named after Moses Cleaveland, who laid out the city as part of a survey in 1796. It is said that the city's name was later shortened when a newspaper editor was unable to fit all the letters in the paper's masthead. The second largest city in Ohio, Cleveland is located where the Cuyahoga River enters Lake Erie. It is a major manufacturing and commercial center and ranks as one of the chief ports on the Great Lakes.

Under its colonial charter, Connecticut claimed northeast Ohio as part of the Western Reserve. In 1795, when Connecticut sold most of the territory, the purchaser—the Connecticut Land Company—sent a party to survey the area. Moses Cleaveland led this party and a settlement was established.

Completion of the Ohio and Erie Canal in 1832 transformed Cleveland from a frontier community to a commercial center at the head of an important waterway. Cleveland now stood on the principal route between the Midwest and the country's urban areas.

Growth was stimulated during the Civil War when demand for iron and steel products was created. This in turn formed the basis for other heavy industries and, by 1900, six major automobile manufacturers were operating in the city. This created vast fortunes for industrialists such as John D. Rockefeller, founder of the Standard Oil Company. The comic book character, Superman, was also developed in Cleveland by two classmates from Glenville High School in the early 1930s.

Cleveland experienced decline in the 1960s with aging industrial plants, high labor costs, population migration, and high racial tensions. In 1978, the city became the first municipality to default on its debts since the Great Depression of the 1930s. Renaissance began in the 1980s with various initiatives including the redevelopment of the Lake Erie shoreline and the construction of the Rock and Roll Hall of Fame.

RIGHT: *Cleveland skyline at dusk: tallest building is Key Tower (947ft) built in 1991; to its right BP Tower (658ft); illuminated is Terminal Tower (708ft) built in 1930.* © CORBIS

FAR RIGHT: *Cleveland is known for its sports: the Browns, the Cavaliers, and the Indians—the latter play at Jacobs Field which opened April 8, 2002.* © William Manning/CORBIS

Indians
SHERWIN-WILLIAMS PAINTS
McDONALD & COMPANY
PEPSI
MTD
Budweiser
OfficeMax

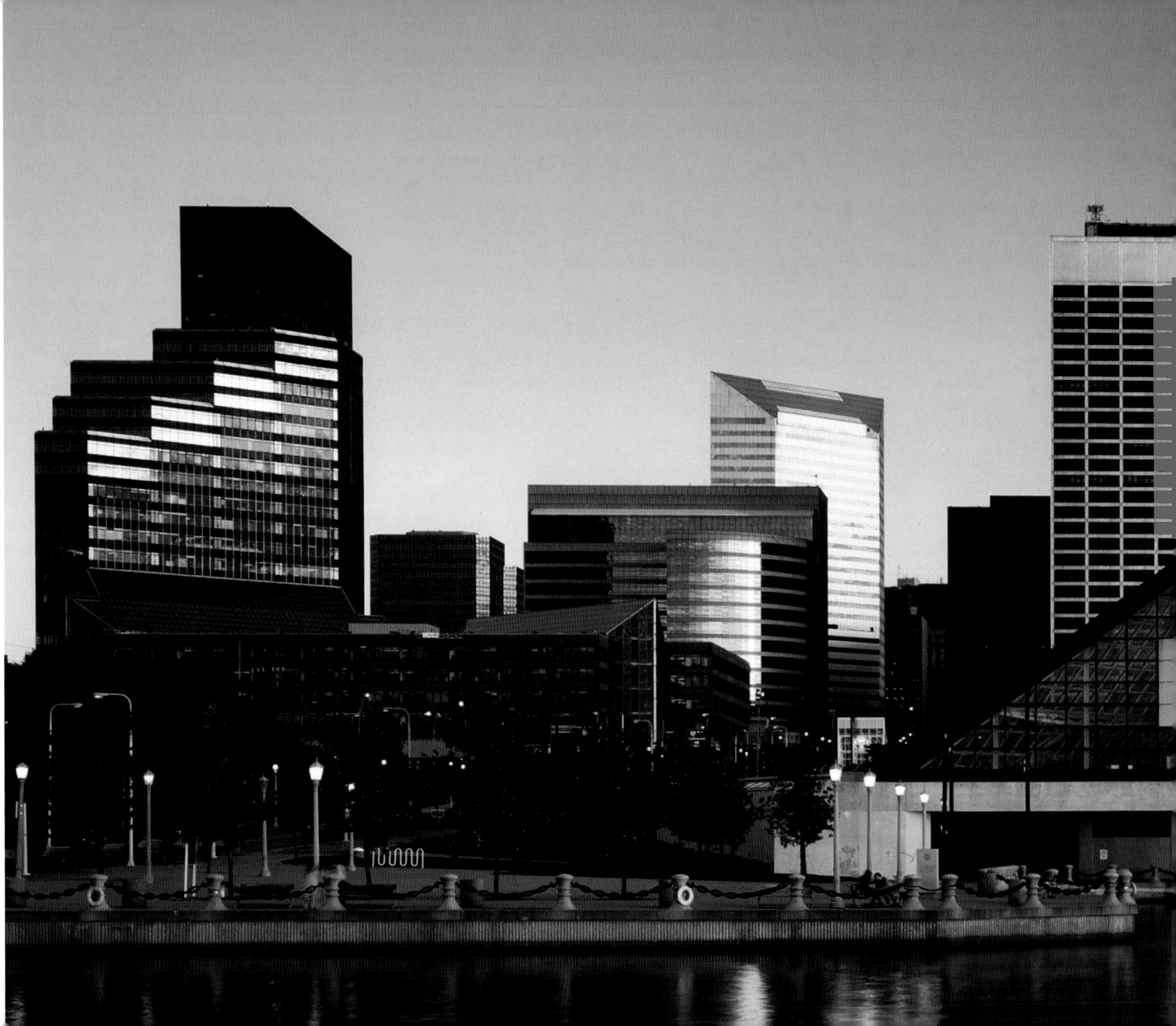

Opened on September 1, 1995, the Rock and Roll Hall of Fame and Museum was designed by I.M. Pei. On the shore of Lake Erie, the building was designed as Pei said, "to echo the energy of rock and roll." It cost $84 million, covers 150,000 square-feet, and is the centerpiece of Cleveland's North Coast Harbor.
© Wes Thompson/CORBIS

COLUMBUS

Location 39.961°N 82.998°W
Area 210.3 square miles
Altitude 800 feet above sea level
City Population 711,470
Time Zone Eastern

Situated where the Scioto and Olentangy rivers meet, Columbus is the largest city and capital of the state of Ohio. Despite a decline in population in the 1980s and early 1990s, it still enjoys a healthy economy. Named after the famed explorer Christopher Columbus (a full-scale replica of his flagship the Santa Maria was built for the 500th anniversary of his Atlantic crossing), it is renowned for businesses operating in information processing, technology, and research as well as manufacturing.

Sited opposite Franklinton (a thriving trade center since 1797), Columbus absorbed this smaller settlement in 1824, eight years after the government offices were moved from Chillicothe, the first state capital. With easy access to transportation, the city thrived throughout the 19th century and the Ohio and Erie Canal passed in close proximity, prompting a short feeder canal to be opened in 1831. This connected Columbus to both Lake Erie and the Ohio River. Then in 1833, the National Road, used by settlers traveling west, reached the city before the railroad finally arrived in 1850.

The Civil War resulted in substantial military activity in Columbus and several army camps were set up, including Camp Chase, the largest military prison for Confederate soldiers.

Manufacturing started in the second half of the 19th Century with the construction of wagons and carriages. This was in part due to the city's location along major routes, while prosperous farmers working the fertile Ohio landscape created a demand for farm vehicles. In 1886, the American Federation of Labor was established in Columbus during a period when workers were fighting for an eight-hour day.

Sustained prosperity over many years has contributed to the high standard of living and relatively crime-free environment that residents take advantage of today, the sympathetically restored German Village district being a particularly sought-after location.

FAR RIGHT: *The neoclassical Ohio Statehouse, built between 1839 and 1861, stands in the state capital of Columbus. The Greek revival capitol, with Doric columns made of native stone, was designed by architect Henry Walter of Cincinnati. Politics took a hand when the legislature repealed the authorization to build in 1840; it would take 20 more years to finish and more architects—William R. West, N.B. Kelly, Thomas U. Walter, Richard Upjohn, and Isaiah Rogers. During this time the original dome was reduced substantially in size.* © Lee Snider/Photo Images/CORBIS

View to the northeast from Bicentennial Park. At left is the William Green Building built in 1990. In the center, the LeVeque Tower was built in 1927. The architect was Charles Howard Crane who designed more than 200 different movie houses and theaters across the U.S. and Canada. To the right of the photograph are the red granite-clad towers of the 1984-built Huntingdon Center and the glass-topped Vern Riffe State Office Tower. Named for Vernal G. Riffe, Jr. who served as Speaker of the Ohio House of Representatives from 1975 to 1994, it includes the 854-seat Capitol Theater. © William Manning/CORBIS

GO JACKETS !
Nationwide

ABOVE: *Architect Howard Dwight Smith designed the horseshoe-shaped, double-deck Ohio Stadium which was completed in time for the 1922 football season. Here, fans of the Ohio State University Buckeyes enter the stadium for the game against the Marshall University Thundering Herd on September 11, 2004. Ohio State defeated Marshall 24–21.* © David Maxwell/Getty Images

LEFT: *A general view of action in the game between the Columbus Blue Jackets and the Detroit Red Wings on December 23, 2002, at Nationwide Arena in Columbus, Ohio. The Red Wings defeated the Blue Jackets 1–0. Founded in 2000, the Blue Jackets is a recent franchise that is hoping to make history.*
© Matthew Stockman/Getty Images/NHLI

FAR LEFT: *Mike Cassidy dances at the 10th Annual New Year's Eve Sobriety Powwow, December 31, 2002/January 1, 2003, in Columbus. The Ohio Center for Native American Affairs sponsored the event, attracting people from several U.S. states as well as Canada. The non-profit making organization was founded in 1975 by Selma Walker, a Dakota from the Yankton Reservation in South Dakota.* © Mike Simons/Getty Images

DALLAS

Location 32.783°N 96.8°W
Area 342.5 square miles
Altitude 463 feet above sea level
City Population 1,188,580
Time Zone Central

Dallas is assured a place in the history books for the world-shaking events of November 22, 1963, when President John F. Kennedy was assassinated. Though Lee Harvey Oswald was arrested for the crime, he was killed by night-club owner Jack Ruby 48 hours later and the conspiracy theories have continued ever since. The Kennedy Memorial, erected in 1970, and the Sixth Floor Museum (1989) enshrine the memory.

Prior to this, the name of John Neely Bryan was the one most often associated with the city, having founded it in 1841 as a trading post on the Trinity River serving Indians and settlers. In 1845, Dallas became part of the state of Texas, was named in 1846 after Vice President George M. Dallas, and with the addition of settlers from nearby La Reunion, boasted a population of 2,000 by 1860. However, a fire in that year destroyed most of the business district.

Just as the arrival of the railroad in 1872 saw the population soar to more than 7,000, so the air age helped Dallas develop. The city became the site of two military facilities at Love Field (later the municipal airport before being replaced by Dallas/Fort Worth in 1974) and Fair Park.

The discovery of oil 100 miles east of Dallas in 1930 shielded the city from the worst effects of the Depression, and would be what it was best known for during the rest of the century as Dallas became the center of operations for oil fields in East Texas, the Gulf Coast, and Oklahoma.

The Texas Centennial Exposition in 1936 saw many buildings built in Fair Park, and an influx of some 10 million visitors, while major growth half a century later saw high-rise office buildings change the city's skyline.

Dallas, whose population topped a million in the late 1980s, began to look more toward its cultural heritage. In 1966, the Dallas County Heritage Society was formed to save Millermore, the last surviving pre-Civil War mansion. Their efforts resulted in the creation of Old City Park. In 1973, Swiss Avenue was designated the city's historic district. The West End, an old warehouse district, opened in the 1980s as a restaurant and entertainment area.

Also in the 1980s, Dallas helped revitalize its downtown through the creation of an arts district incorporating the Dallas Museum of Art (which moved there from Fair Park in 1984) and the Morton H. Meyerson Symphony Center which opened in 1989. The Dallas Cowboys Football team are also a major attraction.

Moon over Dallas. © Bill Ross/CORBIS

FAR LEFT: *The Dallas County Administration Building (formerly the Texas School Book Depository) from which assassin Lee Harvey Oswald shot and killed President John F. Kennedy, November 22, 1963.* © Matt Rourke/AFP/Getty Images

Dallas skyline—looking east. Center, the tallest building at 921ft is Bank of America Plaza, built in 1985; to its left in the photograph, but in fact nearer the viewer, is the 560ft Reunion Tower—a "Spanish-style exclamation point to the far end of the Dallas skyline." To the right of the Bank of America building is the Renaissance Tower, an 886ft high building dating back to 1974. The 1987 Bank One Center is on the right of the photograph. The triangular-topped building at left is Fountain Place designed by Henry Cobb of I.M. Pei & Partners; to its right the Trammell Crow Tower. © Joseph Sohm; ChromoSohm Inc./CORBIS

DENVER

Location 39.739°N 104.984°W
Area 153.4 square miles
Altitude 5,260 feet above sea level
City Population 554,636
Time Zone Mountain Daylight Saving

Denver, "The Mile High City" in the Rocky Mountains, was established in 1858 by gold prospectors where Cherry Creek met the South Platte River. It owed its name to Kansas Governor James W. Denver, Colorado being then a part of that state. Rapid growth with the goldrush led to the establishment of Colorado Territory three years later.

The largest city in Colorado was incorporated in 1861 and made territorial capital in 1867. It soon rivaled San Francisco as the most populous city in the west, with agriculture and manufacturing both enjoying boom times, while gold and silver were discovered in the region in the 1870s. But the depression of 1893 led to diversity into tourism and service industries. The Coors brewery is a notable survivor from this era, and the Colorado Rockies baseball team currently play at Coors Field.

Since the 1940s, Denver has become a major federal center, many citizens being employed by state and local government (only Washington D.C. can claim more). The oil and gas industries have flocked to the area, while other major sources of work include electronics, computers, aviation, and telecommunications: Denver is the nation's largest telecom center.

The 1970s' energy boom saw shopping malls and high-rise office buildings reshape the city skyline but when the price of oil dropped many of these offices fell empty. The city has always been conscious of its relative isolation, and, a year after opening a light-rail transit system, put its money behind a $5 billion airport in 1995 which, at 55 square miles, is the nation's largest.

With ski and mountain resorts, national parks, and frontier historical sites nearby, Denver is also an important tourist center. The former Rocky Mountain Arsenal has become a national wildlife refuge. Academic centers include the University of Denver, and the University of Colorado medical school.

Denver has elected Hispanic (Federico Peña, 1983–91) and African-American (Wellington Webb, 1991–2001) mayors in recent years reflecting its one-third Hispanic, African-American, Asian, and Native American inhabitants.

RIGHT: *Neon artwork at Coors Field.* © Richard Cummins/CORBIS

FAR RIGHT: *Reflections of skyscrapers on a metal sculpture.* © Craig Aurness/CORBIS

At left, the Colorado State Capitol's signature golden dome; the tall white building is Republic Plaza (at 714ft, Denver's tallest); 1801 California Street, the second tallest building in the city (709ft) can be glimpsed just to the left of the 698ft Wells Fargo Center with its russet-colored granite, gray glass, and curving glass roof; to the right the twin towers of the Basilica of the Immaculate Conception, a 1912 example of Gothic architecture.
© Joseph Sohm; Visions of America/CORBIS

DES MOINES

Location 41.600°N 93.608°W
Area 75.8 square miles
Altitude 984 feet above sea level
City Population 193,187
Time Zone Central

Des Moines is the capital of Iowa and seat of Polk County. The city is located in central Iowa where the Des Moines River meets the Raccoon River. As the largest city in the state, it is a major transport, commercial, and manufacturing center.

The fur trade first attracted French explorers to the area and there are several explanations for the name of the city which was incorporated in 1857. It may have been derived from the Native Americans, who traded with the French, from the word for river, *moingwena*,(river of the mounds). Alternatively, it may have come from the French word *moyen* meaning middle because of the site's position midway between the Missouri and Mississippi rivers, or from the French *des moines* meaning monks, for the French missionaries in the area at the time.

Earlier in 1843, Fort Des Moines was built at the junction of the Des Moines and Raccoon rivers by the federal government. The Native Americans gave up their rights to the land some two years later and the area around the fort was opened up to settlers who incorporated the town as Fort Des Moines in 1851. Subsequently, the towns of Fort Des Moines and East Des Moines were merged and incorporated as Des Moines. That same year, the state capital was moved from Iowa City to Des Moines. During the 1950s a major urban-renewal program was started. Extensive damage followed the floods of 1993, but recovery was swift when flood protection measures were introduced, including flood gates and the installation of back-up power systems.

Des Moines has many educational and cultural centers along with recreational facilities. Two notable attractions are the reconstruction of an early 20th-century Iowa community and the Des Moines Botanical Center which houses one of the largest collections of tropical plants in the Midwest.

RIGHT AND BELOW: *The postmodern EMC Insurance Building was constructed in 1997. The city's latest skyscraper is 325ft tall—Des Moines' seventh tallest—some 300ft lower than 801 Grand, the tallest building in Iowa.* © Wes Thompson/CORBIS

FAR RIGHT: *Iowa's State Capitol building is modeled on Napoleon's memorial, Les Invalides, in Paris. Designed by French architect A. Piquenard, who also designed the Illinois State Capitol, it was built in 1884 with a dome that is 274ft high and sits in 85 acres of parkland.* © Joseph Sohm; ChromoSohm Inc./CORBIS

Skyline of Des Moines. The EMC building is at left; next to it, the HUB Tower; in the center Des Moines' tallest building, 801 Grand. © Tom Bean/CORBIS

FAR RIGHT: *The Governor's Mansion, Terrace Hill, was built for Benjamin Franklin Allen, Iowa's first millionaire, between 1866 and 1869. The "Palace of the Prairie"—an 18,000-square-foot home—was designed by a popular Chicago architect of the time, William Boyington.* © Joseph Sohm; ChromoSohm Inc./CORBIS

DETROIT

Location 42.331°N 83.045°W
Area 4,465 square miles
Altitude 600 feet above sea level
City Population 951,270
Time Zone Eastern

Founded in 1701, Detroit was completely destroyed by fire in 1805 but was quickly rebuilt. The home of the motor industry—Chrysler, Ford, and General Motors—Detroit is nevertheless a beautiful city full of museums and sights. However, being located in the northern United States it is freezing cold in winter and unbearably humid in high summer when on July 4 fireworks light the sky as the International Freedom Festival celebrates Independence Day. Then, in September one of the country's most prestigious jazz festivals, the Montreux Detroit Jazz Festival, is held over five days.

A few miles north of downtown is the Cultural Center, a cluster of world-class galleries and museums. The collection of the Detroit Institute of Arts spans 5,000 years, but its main treasure is a Diego Rivera mural called *Detroit Industry*, which takes up all four walls of a large interior garden court. Rivera painted the 27 fresco panels in 1932 to depict the auto industry and contrast the area's natural resources with its factories. The Detroit Historical Museum, a couple of doors away, describes Detroit's earlier days.

Detroit was an important station along the Underground Railroad, a rough and tumble network of escape routes used by abolitionists and African-American slaves who traveled from America's southern states, through the U.S. north, and into Canada. The Second Baptist Church of Detroit was the city's first African-American church and served as a leading "station" on the Underground Railroad in the mid-1800s. Today it gives tours of the crawl spaces where the slaves were hidden on their journey. The Museum of African American History is the world's largest African-American historical and cultural museum with exhibits, classes, a library, and a theater.

Detroit is the home of Motown, a recording label started by Detroiter Berry Gordy Jr., in 1959, naming it after his city's loose way of shortening its "Motor City" moniker. The sign above his new company reads "Hitsville USA" and the hits—by artists like Smokey Robinson, Marvin Gaye, the Temptations and the Supremes—kept on coming. The original recording studio is now a museum, Motown having moved to the West Coast in the 1970s.

RIGHT: *Detroit's Renaissance Center was constructed in the late 1970s. There are seven skyscrapers, the tallest of which is the Marriott Renaissance Center, at 726ft Detroit's tallest building.*
© Alan Schein Photography/CORBIS

BELOW: *Detroit skyline—at left the Renaissance Center. The Penobscot Building, Detroit's tallest building for nearly half a century until the Renaissance Center was built and the eighth largest building in the world in 1928, is in the center of the photograph to the right of the browny-orange Guardian Building. The bridge in the foreground spanning the Detroit River is the Belle-Isle Bridge—the General MacArthur Bridge—built in 1923 and refurbished in the 1980s. It has 19 spans and a length of 2,356ft.* © W. Cody/CORBIS

INSET: *A classic car cruises down Woodward Avenue during the Annual Woodward Dream Cruise in Royal Oak, a suburb of Detroit. The cruise is the largest one-day auto event in the world and draws more than a 1.5 million visitors and approximately 30,000 classic cars.* © Bill Pugliano/Getty Images

View of Downtown Detroit from Windsor. The Renaissance Center is on the right; in the center Detroit's second tallest building, One Detroit Center (619ft) built in 1992. Also known as the Comerica Tower, it is Michigan's tallest office tower and won the Award of Excellence for design in 1996.
© Joseph Sohm; Visions of America/CORBIS

EL PASO

Location 31.758°N 106.486°W
Area 249.1 square miles
Altitude 3,710 feet above sea level
City Population 563,662
Time Zone Mountain Daylight Saving

Situated at the far west tip of Texas where New Mexico and the Mexican state of Chihuahua meet, El Paso was named by Spanish settlers approaching the two mountain ranges who named it El Paso del Norte (the Pass of the North) in 1581. By the 18th century about 5,000 people lived in the area, a dam and a system of irrigation ditches facilitating agriculture in this desert region: El Paso's vineyards remain well respected today.

El Paso fell under Mexican rule when they gained independence from Spain in 1821, but the United States and Mexico went to war in 1846 and two years later the boundary between the nations was fixed at the Rio Grande, the Gila River, and the Colorado River, thence westward to the Pacific. All territory north of that line, known as the Mexican Cession and comprising half of Mexico, became a part of the United States, which paid Mexico $15 million for it. Though now in Texas, El Paso was to be both bicultural and bilingual. (A minor border dispute in 1963 saw a small area of the city transferred to Mexico.)

The arrival of the railroad in 1881–82 overnight turned El Paso into an important frontier community, housing some 10,000 inhabitants by 1890. But the establishment of saloons, dancehalls, gambling dens, and brothels earned it an unwanted reputation. In 1905, the city authorities closed houses of gambling and prostitution. Prohibition brought a tourist boom as Americans took advantage of the drinking and gambling establishments across the border.

As the 20th century progressed, El Paso transformed itself into a modern industrial and commercial center. By 1925 its population exceeded 77,000, the figure including refugees fleeing the Mexican Revolution. The American Smelting and Refining Company remained a major employer into the 1980s, while Standard Oil and Phelps Dodge established petroleum refineries. The city is also today a commercial, industrial, and financial center.

Military matters gained in importance during the Second World War, with Fort Bliss a significant employer. This has continued, and in 1986 military personnel made up a quarter of the city's population. Textiles, tourism, building materials, metals, petroleum, and food processing were El Paso's major industries in 1980.By 1990 the city's population exceeded half a million, with over 50 percent of citizens boasting Spanish surnames.

RIGHT: *Downtown El Paso and its suburban areas, with Ciudad Juarez, Mexico, in the distance. The tall central building is Wells Fargo Plaza, built in 1971.* © Gerald French/CORBIS

FAR RIGHT: *A special agent for Union Pacific Railroad Co. checks a train for signs of theft or illegal riders as it arrives in El Paso.* © Joe Raedle/Newsmakers

LEFT: *First used as a refugee camp in 1675 for Pueblo indians who were escaping Apache raiders, the Spanish settled Tigua Indian refugees of the Pueblo Revolt at Ysleta in 1680. Established by Antonio de Otermín and Fray Francisco de Ayeta in 1682, Corpus Christi de la Ysleta was the first mission and pueblo in Texas. To the Tiguas, the mission church is known as San Antonio, after their patron saint, and they call the pueblo Ysleta del Sur. The present church was constructed in 1851. Its distinctive silver-domed bell tower was added in 1897. In 1907, the mission suffered its last disaster, when a fire destroyed the roof and the bell tower. In 1980, 300 years after the arrival of the Tiguas, the mission's name was changed back to "Misión San Antonio de los Tiguas." The church serves the community of Ysleta and is the second oldest continuously used church in the United States.* © Richard Cummins/CORBIS

BELOW: *Downtown El Paso through the leaves of a giant yucca.* © Jan Butchofsky-Houser/CORBIS

FORT WORTH

Location 32.725°N 97.32°W
Area 292.5 square miles
Altitude 612 feet above sea level
City Population 534,694
Time Zone Central

The U.S. Army established Fort Worth in 1849 as one of a line of ten posts in the state built to protect U.S.-held territory from the Comanche tribe. Settlers and traders soon arrived in numbers and in 1856, after the departure of the army, the settlement became the seat of Tarrant County. During the Civil War, Fort Worth once again became a frontier outpost. After the hostilities, the settlement began to grow and became a meeting place for cowboys and cattle buyers, as well as a starting point for driving longhorn cattle to Kansas.

Incorporated in 1873, Fort Worth is located on the Clear Fork of the Trinity River in the north of Texas. It is a major road, rail, and air junction, as well as a manufacturing and processing center with a diverse economy and is named after General William Jenkins Worth, a hero of the Mexican War (1846–48).

By 1876, the fort had become the east terminus for the Texas and Pacific Railroad. Farming, especially cattle, continued to dominate Fort Worth's economy and in the early 20th century the city built stockyards and became the principal slaughterhouse, packing, and shipping point for livestock in the state.

With the discovery of oil during the early 1900s, Fort Worth became a major player in the manufacture of oil exploration and extraction equipment and several petroleum companies chose the city as their base. Disastrous flooding of Trinity River in 1909 prompted attempts to control the river and, as a result, Lake Worth was created.

During World War II, the city attracted military bases and federal funds were eventually secured which were used to build the Trinity River Floodway, completed in 1956. After years of decline, Fort Worth began a program of revitalization which also included the creation of several green belt areas, and the city continues to thrive thoughtfully today.

LEFT: *At far right the City Center Towers built in 1982–84 (City Center Tower II is 547ft; the Chase Texas Tower is 477ft), then Carter and Burgess Plaza (525ft) built in 1983; in the center is the Landmark Tower (380ft) also known as Continental National Bank Building, which was built in 1957. The tallest building in Fort Worth is Burnett Plaza at 567ft.* © Danny Lehman/CORBIS

RIGHT: *Sundance Square—named for the Sundance Kid, who hid out here with the Hole-in-the-Wall Gang—is the heart of downtown nightlife in Fort Worth, 20 blocks of historic buildings, unique stores, art galleries, and museums.* © Danny Lehman/CORBIS

RIGHT: *Fort Worth Stockyards Historic District was designated as an historic landmark in 1976. It covers 125 acres where you can see the world's only daily cattle drive, hear live country stars, drink in an authentic saloon, or enjoy one of the regular annual festivals, such as the Chisholm Trail Roundup in June or Pioneer Days in September.* © Gerald French/CORBIS

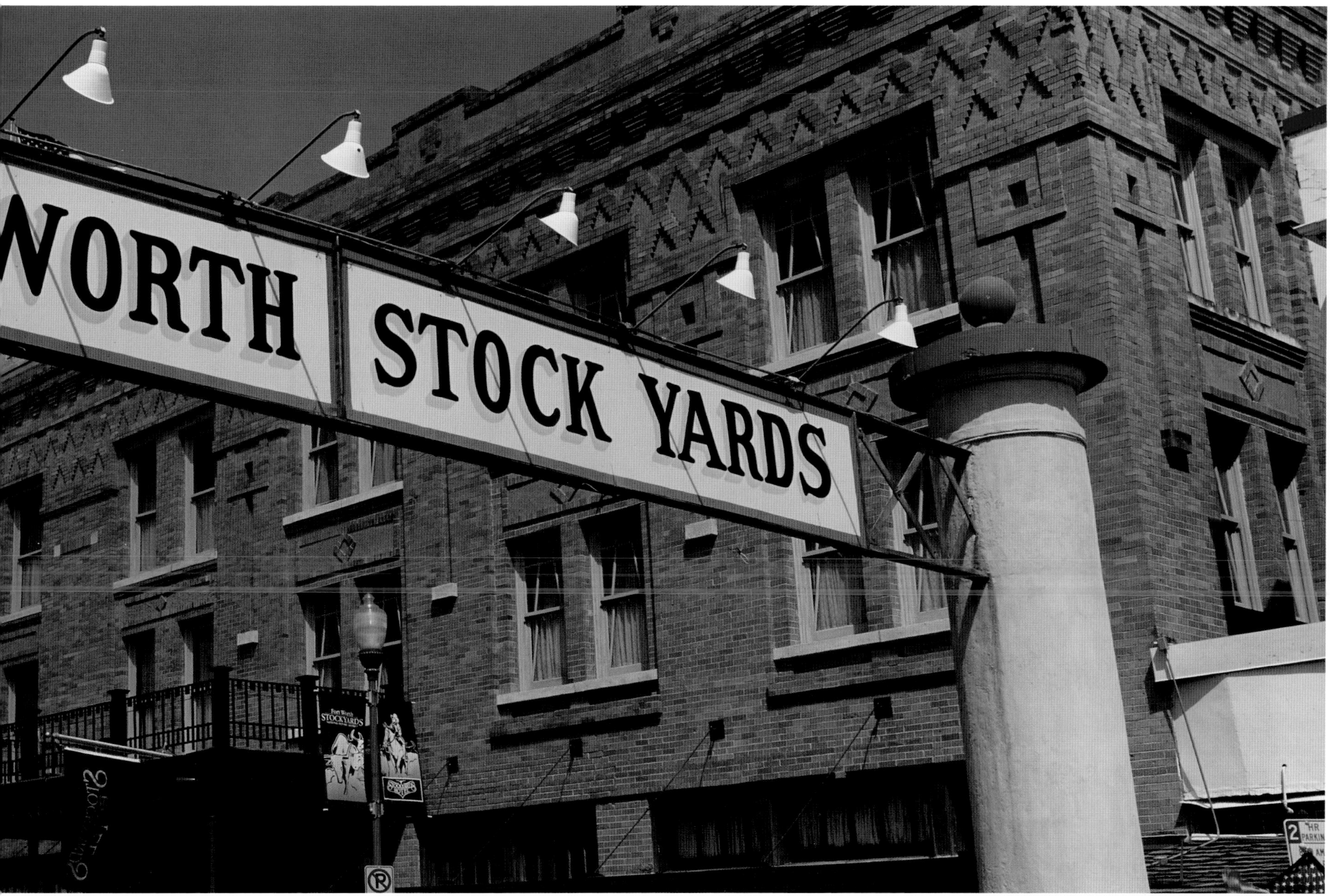
WORTH STOCK YARDS
Fort Worth
STOCKYARDS

FRESNO

Location 36.747°N 119.771°W
Area 104.4 square miles
Altitude 296 feet above sea level
City Population 427,652
Time Zone Pacific Daylight Saving

Renowned for being the raisin-producing capital of the world, Fresno is the seat of Fresno County in central California located at the hub of the state's fertile San Joaquin Valley, one of the richest farming areas in the United States. The name Fresno, meaning "ash tree" in Spanish, was first applied to the Fresno River where such trees were seen growing along its banks. In 1872, a settlement grew up near to the river and was named Fresno when the Central Pacific Railroad founded it as a station.

There is evidence to suggest that people have lived in the area for at least 8,000 years but the Yokuts were the sole inhabitants until the mid-19th century when the California Goldrush began and the first white settlers (the "Forty-Niners") arrived. Fresno County was established in 1856, but the city was not founded until the arrival of the railroad. The first irrigation system took advantage of the area's rich agricultural land in 1876 and local citizens voted to incorporate the city in 1885.

During the 20th century the city grew steadily and, by 1910, was the scene of a labor dispute led by the radical Industrial Workers of the World. The editor of the *Fresno Morning Republican*, Chester H Rowell, became one of the leaders of the progressive reform movement. The 1950s saw Fresno as the nation's leading agricultural country and during the 1990s the city was challenged by a massive growth in population.

Local farmers grow more than 250 different crops, including cotton, grapes, tomatoes, almonds, garlic, oranges, and nectarines. Fresno and surrounding areas grow around 60 percent of the world's raisins and more than 90 percent of raisins sold on the U.S. market. More recently, the economy has expanded to include manufacturing, service, and industrial operations.

RIGHT: *The remarkable Fresno City Hall was designed in 1987 by Arthur Erickson. It is a five-story, 201,750-square-foot structure that uses externally a metallic trim in sea-foam green; the roof is comprised of two acres of stainless steel.* © Richard Cummins/CORBIS

FAR RIGHT: *The Meux Home Museum recaptures the flavor of Victorian Fresno. Built in 1888, it has been owned and maintained by the city since 1970. The house boasts dozens of custom features and a fascinating collection.* © Mark E. Gibson/CORBIS

OVERLEAF, LEFT: *The famous arch at the south end of Van Ness Avenue welcomes visitors to Fresno.* © Robert Holmes/CORBIS

OVERLEAF, RIGHT: *The Fresno Veterans Memorial Auditorium was built by Swartz & Ryland and houses the Legion of Valor Museum. © Richard Cummins/CORBIS*

FRESNO
THE BEST LITTLE CITY IN THE U.S.A.
VAN NESS AVE
ENTRANCE
SPEED LIMIT 30

FRESNO MEMORIAL AUDITORIUM
2425

HONOLULU

Location 21.306°N 157.858°W
Area 85.7 square miles
Altitude 18 feet above sea level
City Population 371,657
Time Zone Hawaiian Time Zone

Capital and largest city of the state of Hawaii, its name means "sheltered bay" or "place of shelter." It first became accepted as the capital of the island in 1809 when Kamehameha, ruler of the Hawaiian islands from 1795, moved his court from Waikiki to Honolulu Harbor, then little more than a village of some 1,800 inhabitants.

Honolulu quickly grew in both size and stature, serving as a stopping-off point for the numerous whaling ships working the Pacific Ocean in need of supplies, liquor, and women. This in turn led to numerous bars and brothels opening in the harbor area, closely followed by the arrival of Christian missionaries, who quickly ingratiated themselves with the royal family. Indeed, when one missionary nursed the sick Queen Kaahumanu back to health, Kamehameha showed his gratitude by passing a law forbidding work and travel on the Sabbath.

This civilizing influence soon saw the number of taverns and brothels fall, with the whalers in consequence preferring to frequent less stringent towns. Yet in their absence Honolulu still grew in importance, with the establishment of a Supreme Court and numerous corporations opening their headquarters in the city. The monarchy in Hawaii came to an end with the death of King David Kalakaua in 1891; the various debts he had amassed during his reign had made him unpopular with the sugar barons on the island and, although the king's sister Queen Liliuokalani was about to announce a new constitution, the monarchy was overthrown and the American flag hoisted above the capitol.

U.S. President Grover Cleveland ordered it to be taken down and the monarchy restored, but he was ignored and the subsequent Spanish-American War of 1898, which resulted in the acquisition of the Philippines, saw American expansion in the area continue. President McKinley adopted the annexation of the islands and appointed a governor in 1900, although Hawaii did not become a fully-fledged U.S. state until 1959.

RIGHT: *Waikiki Beach and Honolulu seen from the east with Diamond Head behind the photographer. There are 64 buildings over 300ft tall in the area.* © Randy Faris/CORBIS

FAR RIGHT: *The $95 million Kalia Tower opened in 2001. It was Waikiki's first all-steel-framed hotel tower and has 453 guest rooms and suites. It has reopened following being closed for much of 2003 because of mold.* © Phil Mislinski/Getty Images

LEFT: *Honolulu skyline.*
© Randy Faris/CORBIS

HOUSTON

Location 29.763°N 95.363°W
Area 579.4 square miles
Altitude 40 feet above sea level
City Population 1,953,631
Time Zone Central

The fourth largest city in the United States, Houston has enjoyed growth throughout the last hundred or so years, making it known as both the "fastest-growing city in America" and "the most popular city to Relocate to." Following the Texas Revolution in 1836 New York property developers John Kirby Allen and Augustus Chapman Allen bought over 6,500 acres of land to form the site of a city that they were to name after Sam Houston, the hero of San Jacinto (a major battle in the Texas Revolution) and a man the Allen brothers saw as potentially the first President of the Republic of Texas.

Houston began as little more than a hamlet but grew quickly and in little less than a year had been incorporated as a city. It was also temporarily made capital of Texas, but the lawlessness that overtook the city saw that status eventually move to Austin (it would temporarily return in 1842 when Mexico again threatened invasion). The same year saw work begin on the port of Houston and over the next decade rail links were established that enabled various industries to set up base there, including cotton, lumber, and iron. A fire ravaged the city in 1859, but Houston was soon rebuilt.

After admittance into the United States as a slave state in 1846, it was estimated that nearly 50 percent of the population was enslaved. At the end of the Civil War and following four years of military rule in Texas by the Unionists, Houston set about restructuring itself, and after Texas rejoined the Union in 1870 Houston was accepted as a port of entry. Houston requested permission to become a deepwater port in 1898 following the threat of the Spanish-American War, and this was approved the following year. A year later, in 1900, a hurricane hit Galveston and scared investment away from that city into Houston, which rapidly grew, especially with the discovery of oil in Texas in 1901—by 1913, a dozen oil companies were headquartered in Houston.

Perhaps the most important industry to have been drawn to the city is aeronautics, with the opening of the Manned Spacecraft Center at Clear Lake City (now a suburb of Houston), now named the Lyndon B. Johnson Space Center. It was here that the first manned landing on the moon in 1969 was masterminded, and indeed the first word spoken by a man on the lunar surface was "Houston" as Neil Armstrong reported back their safe landing. This historic series of events has led to Houston being named "Space City," although it is also known as "Bayou City," "Clutch City," and "Magnolia City."

FAR LEFT: *The simplicity of the Saint John Evangelical Lutheran Church in Sam Houston Historical Park stands in stark contrast to the skyscrapers rising behind it—the Texaco Heritage Plaza (762ft) immediately behind, Wells Fargo Plaza (972ft) to its left, and One Shell Plaza (714ft) with its tall aerial at far left.* © Lowell Georgia/CORBIS

LEFT: *Houston will be forever linked with oil and space: NASA has controlled its missions from here since 1965. Here Astronaut Tamara E. Jernigan takes part in an underwater space walk simulation at the Johnson Space Center, Houston.* © NASA/Getty Images

OVERLEAF: *Downtown Houston at the turn of the 21st century. Note the stepped Bank of America Center (772ft) at left and stepped Continental Center I (732ft) at right. These two were built in 1983 and 1984 respectively: eight of the tallest ten buildings in Houston were built in the 1980s.* © Joseph Sohm; Visions of America/CORBIS

AllenCenter Parking

INDIANAPOLIS

Location 39.768°N 86.158°W
Area 361.5 square miles
Altitude 717 feet above sea level
City Population 781,870
Time Zone Eastern Standard

The 12th largest city in the United States and the state capital of Indiana, Indianapolis was founded in 1822, on the White River, although there had been settlements in the area for some six years previously. In 1820 ten commissioners appointed by the Indiana General Assembly gathered at the point where Fall Creek met the White River and recommended that this should be the site of the new state capital.

While the river was undoubtedly an important reason for siting Indianapolis at that spot, in reality it was too shallow in places and the shores too sandy, necessitating the building of a canal so that goods could be brought to the city center. In time this Central Canal would link with the Wabash River, which ran to the north and west of the capital, and ultimately the canals in Ohio, thus making Indianapolis an important trade route. Work on the canals took longer than expected, largely because the State of Indiana was declared bankrupt after a series of bad investments!

Rail connections also became an important factor in allowing the city to enlarge and at the turn of the 20th century, the automobile was to see an explosion of development within Indianapolis. A number of manufacturers headquartered in the city, including Deusenburg, Marmon, National, and Stutz, making Indianapolis a serious rival to Detroit in the production stakes, although almost all these names have long since disappeared.

The major link Indianapolis retains with its automotive past is the famed Indianapolis 500, an annual race that was first held in the city in 1911, although racing at the site at French Lick had begun two years previously (in that first race, part of the track surface broke up, resulting in the deaths of two drivers, two mechanics, and two spectators). Site owner Carl Graham Fisher thereafter decided on a much grander single extravaganza which would ultimately become the Indy 500.

RIGHT: *Indiana State Capitol building at dusk. This beautifully restored Renaissance Revival Statehouse was built 1878–88.* © Joseph Sohm; Visions of America/CORBIS

FAR RIGHT: *The National Collegiate Athletic Association's Hall of Champions was designed by architect Michael Graves. Situated in White River State Park it represents all 23 sports administered by the organization: Baseball , Basketball, Cross Country, Diving, Fencing, Field Hockey, Football, Golf, Gymnastics, Ice Hockey, Lacrosse, Rifle, Rowing, Skiing, Soccer, Softball, Swimming, Tennis, Track and Field, Volleyball, Water Polo, and Wrestling.* © Mark E. Gibson/CORBIS

NCAA
HALL OF

VIAGRA
ups
DU PONT
MONTE CARLO

FAR LEFT: *Indianapolis skyline at dusk. In the center Indianapolis's tallest building at 811ft, Bank One Tower—built in 1990 it is the tallest building in Indiana, and the tallest in the Midwest outside Chicago and Cleveland; at left OneAmerica Tower, built in 1982, Indianapolis's second tallest at 533ft.* © Richard Cummins/CORBIS

LEFT: *Indianapolis is best known to the rest of the world for racing. The pace car was called out for a record 13 times during the NASCAR Nextel Cup Series Brickyard 400 on August 8, 2004, at Indianapolis Motor Speedway.* © Gavin Lawrence/Getty Images

BELOW: *A 1985 aerial view of the Indy 500 race site.* © Bettmann/CORBIS

JACKSONVILLE

Location 30.331°N 81.655°W
Area 757.7 square miles
Altitude 12 feet above sea level
City Population 735,617
Time Zone Eastern

Jacksonville is one of the south's more culturally rewarding cities, despite its gray, industrial exterior, and is the largest conurbation in the state of Florida. The surrounding area contains beaches, parks, and woodland areas, offering ready availability of water-based leisure pursuits.

The city was settled by French Huguenots in the mid-16th century at the mouth of the St John's River. It was originally known as Fort Caroline, and after the original military settlement (now the Fort Caroline National Memorial) was taken by the Spanish, a city developed around it in 1816–22. This was renamed after U.S. President Andrew Jackson who, prior to making the White House, was the first territorial governor of Florida.

The city's favored climatic conditions made it a thriving tourist resort for those seeking winter sunshine after the end of the Civil War (it also has a significant retired community), but the combination of a yellow fever outbreak in 1888 and the Great Fire in 1901 killed the tourist trade, though the city was quickly rebuilt: hence 20th century Jacksonville's preoccupation with commerce and industry.

The 1920s saw the New York film industry move south and make Jacksonville its base, while water-borne trade such as timber, fruit, phosphates, and tobacco, facilitated by the development of a deep-water harbor, added to the city's growing prosperity. The city is also a major U.S. Navy port; the service runs three important installations in the area, including Jacksonville Naval Air Station and the large Mayport base.

Culturally, Jacksonville is a multi-faceted experience, with a major jazz festival held in the Metropolitan Park each October. There's also the World Golf Hall of Fame, the Confederate Monument in Hemming Park, and the nearby Fort Caroline National Memorial.

RIGHT: *Alltel Stadium and Jacksonville skyline. On August 18, 1995, the Jacksonville Jaguars played their first ever NFL game in their new stadium, built faster than any major-league stadium in 19 and a half months.* © Alan Schein Photography/CORBIS

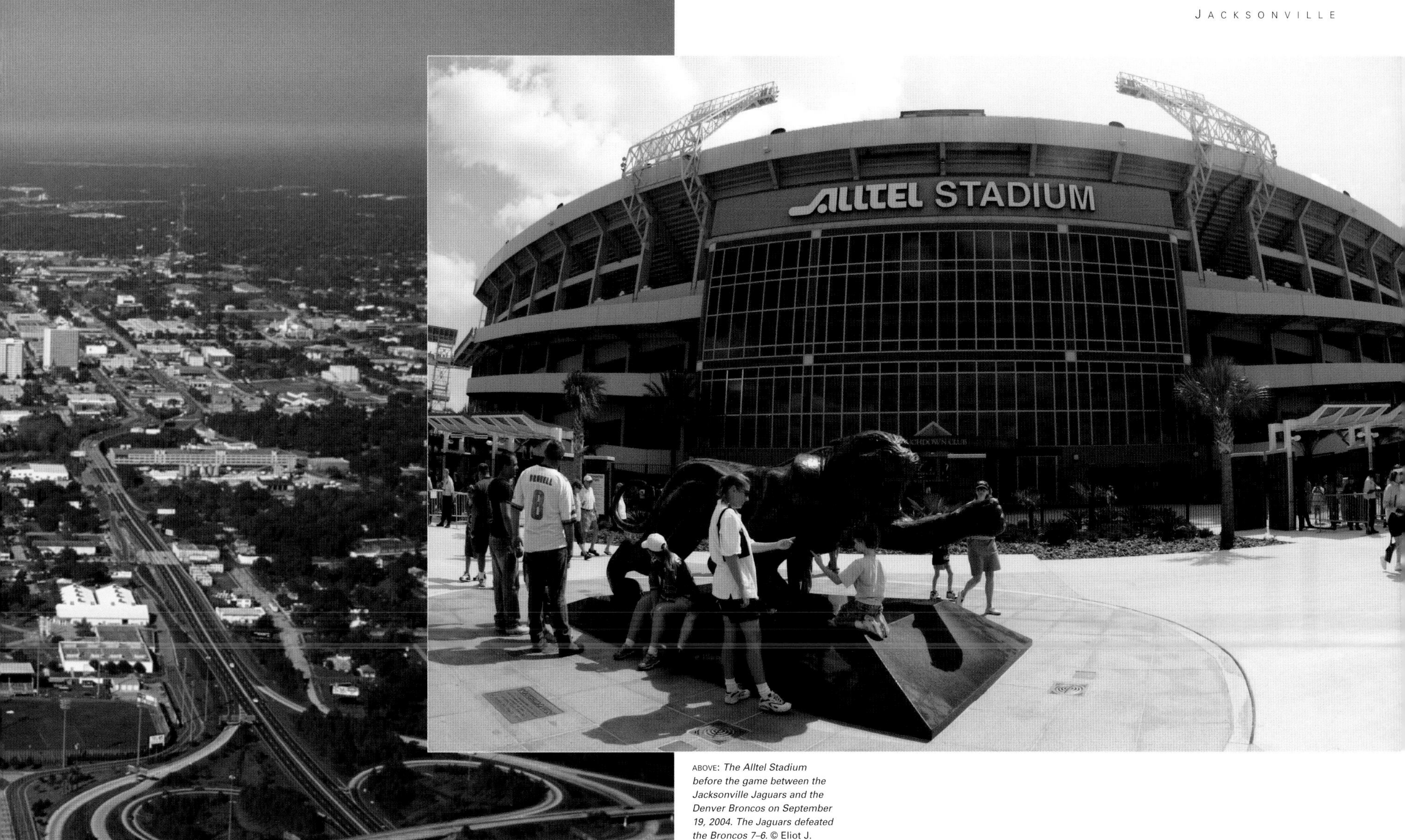

ABOVE: *The Alltel Stadium before the game between the Jacksonville Jaguars and the Denver Broncos on September 19, 2004. The Jaguars defeated the Broncos 7–6.* © Eliot J. Schechter/Getty Images

BELLSOUTH

LEFT: *The Friendship Fountain in Downtown Jacksonville. One of the world's tallest fountains, it shoots water more than 120ft. Behind can be seen the two tallest buildings in the city: the 535ft Modis Tower and, to its left, the Bank of America Tower (617ft).*
© Mark E. Gibson/CORBIS

KANSAS CITY

Location 39.099°N 94.578°W
Area 313.5 square miles
Altitude 882 feet above sea level
City Population 441,545
Time Zone Central

Frenchman Francois Chouteau, from St. Louis, is credited with being the first non-native American to settle in the area that is now Kansas City, arriving in 1821 and setting up a trading post on the Missouri River. He was flooded out in 1826 and re-established his trading post on higher ground further up the river, being joined by several other French families. In 1831 members of the Church of Jesus Christ of Latter-Day Saints, more commonly known as Mormons, coming from areas such as Ohio and New York State, purchased nearly 2,000 acres of land in the Paseo and Troost Lake areas of Missouri. Two years later, after a series of disagreements between the Yankee Saints and southern Missourians, the Mormons were expelled from the county.

At about the same time a dock was established on the Missouri River in order to land supplies for Westport Landing. The land surrounding the dock was purchased by the Town Company in 1838 and the following year Westport Landing was renamed the Town of Kansas, after local Kansa Indians. The town became the City of Kansas in 1853, the same year the first municipal election was held (a total of 67 voters from a population of approximately 2,500). Over the next 30 years, the population swelled to more than 60,000 and a decision was taken to rename the conurbation Kansas City.

In its early years Kansas City was an important cattle trading center, with one of America's largest cattle markets, an industry that peaked in the early 20th century. From 1915 to 1940 the city was run by one man, Tom Pendergast, a businessman who gave workers jobs and helped elect politicians (he was instrumental in getting future U.S. President Harry S. Truman a post as county judge at Jackson County, Missouri, an appointment that would taint Truman with accusations that he was corrupt) in return for favors; his Ready-Mixed Concrete company won many government contracts, often without the need for tenders. Pendergast was eventually jailed for failing to pay taxes on a bribe and the crime wave that had accompanied his control of the city began to subside. Today Kansas City has been described as "the right city in the right place at the right time."

LEFT: *Kansas City skyscrapers aglow at dusk. The tallest structures are, left to right, the Town Pavilion (591ft), One Kansas City Place (at 632ft the tallest building in the city; the tallest structure is the KC TV tower at 1,042ft), the Kansas City Power & Light Building and the Art Deco pylons topping the Bartle Hall Convention Center. At 491ft, the Power and Light Building is a high spot for Art Deco in a city that ranks among America's top ten for Art Deco buildings. Built in 1931, its crowning pillar of changing colored lights is 97ft high and designed to symbolize electric power. There are no windows on the west facade because an identical twin tower was to be added. The Depression forced the plans to be abandoned.* © Richard Cummins/CORBIS

ABOVE: *Flamingo paddleboat casino along the Missouri River.* © Richard Cummins/CORBIS

OVERLEAF: *View of Kansas City from the south. At right, the Crown Center, a collection of buildings the highest of which is the Hyatt Regency (504ft), built in 1980.* © Joseph Sohm; Visions of America/CORBIS

MIDWEST
HOTEL
BELGER
Cartage Service, Inc.
MOTOR INN HOTEL

LAS VEGAS

Location 36.175°N 115.136°W
Area 113.3 square miles
Altitude 2,000 feet above sea level
City Population 478,434
Time Zone Pacific Daylight Saving

Since the name Las Vegas has become synonymous with gambling and the activities of legendary crime lords, there has always been the notion that Las Vegas is a recent development. Not so, for Mormon farmers first came to the area in 1854, with the town having already been named by Spaniards of the Antonio Armijo party who had stopped in the area for water while heading along the Old Spanish Trail to Texas. The name derives from the Spanish for "fertile valleys" and acknowledges the fact that the area around Las Vegas contained artesian springs that enabled extensive green areas to crop up in an area that was largely desert.

Although the Mormons abandoned the area in 1857, a fort (Fort Baker) was built here in 1864, since the presence of springs enabled Las Vegas to become a water stop for wagon trains and, later, the railroads on the route to California and New Mexico. Las Vegas was founded in 1905 and incorporated in 1911. With the legalization of gambling in 1931 the area began to attract considerable interest and investment, a small trickle becoming a torrent in the early 1940s when numerous hotels and casinos began opening up in the city.

It is widely believed that the likes of notorious criminals such as Benjamin "Bugsy" Siegel and Meyer Lansky were the organizers of this explosion of investment, initially as a way of laundering their criminal proceeds from various sources and then as a money-making scheme all of its own. Las Vegas soon acquired a nickname that summed up its activities, "Sin City," although the local government has long favored "The Entertainment Capital of the World." Similarly, while local government has attempted to attract industries into the city that are not connected to its past (with some success, the lack of state, individual, or corporate income tax having brought light manufacturing industries to the city), there is no escaping the fact that it is legalized gambling, drinking, and adult entertainment that continues to draw many to a city that is the largest in Nevada and one of the fastest-growing urban areas in the United States.

RIGHT: *The view north from the MGM Grand of hotels on the Las Vegas Strip, including (left to right) the Bellagio, The Mirage, Paris, and the Aladdin.* © Richard Cummins/CORBIS

ABOVE: *A welcome sign greets visitors at the entrance to Las Vegas.*
© Ann Johansson/CORBIS

OVERLEAF: *An aerial view of the hotels on Las Vegas Boulevard. The wide street in the center left is the Strip. On the left, starting at the bottom, is the Sahara, and farther on, the Flamingo, Baileys, and colored lights of the Excalibur. On the right, the white building at bottom is Circus Circus, the building with the diagonal color scheme is the Stardust; farther off are Treasure Island and the Mirage. The red building in the right distance is the Rio.*
© Joseph Sohm; Visions of America/CORBIS

Bank of America
STARDUST

STARDUST

LONG BEACH

Location 33.766°N 118.188°W
Area 50.4 square miles
Altitude 29 feet above sea level
City Population 461,522
Time Zone Pacific Daylight Saving

Given its close proximity to Los Angeles, it has always been assumed that Long Beach is merely a suburb of the former. This is not so, for there are 20 or so miles that separate Long Beach and downtown Los Angeles.

Long Beach was originally founded as Willmore City in 1880 and incorporated as a city in 1888 as a seaside resort (no doubt many Los Angeles' inhabitants would flock to Long Beach for the weekend), with The Pike becoming a famous amusement park in the city from 1910 for the next 50 or so years. It later grew as an oil, U.S. Navy, and port town, and it is this latter function that has enabled Long Beach to become the second busiest seaport in the United States. A total of $100 billion-worth of cargo is loaded and unloaded in the Port of Long Beach each year, some 70 million metric tons of goods! A former naval shipyard is being converted to a commercial drydock and shipping terminal, while high-technology and aerospace industries have made their home in the area.

Like many other West Coast cities, Long Beach has suffered from the occasional earthquake, the last major occurrence being the 6.3 (Richter Scale) magnitude earthquake that struck the city in 1933. Those buildings built out of unreinforced masonry, especially schools, suffered the worst damage and there were 120 fatalities.

In more recent times, Long Beach has become the permanent home of the RMS *Queen Mary*, the former Cunard liner that operated in the North Atlantic between 1936 and 1967. Since being retired and moored in Long Beach, the *Queen Mary* has become a hotel, museum, and major tourist attraction. Other attractions in the city include the Aquarium of the Pacific and the Grand Prix of Long Beach, an IndyCar event that actually takes place through the streets of the city.

RIGHT: *Californian sunset at Long Beach.*
© Robert Landau/CORBIS

An aerial view of Long Beach, California, shows the Long Beach Downtown Marina, Queensway Bay, and Shore Line Park. © Douglas Slone/CORBIS

FAR LEFT: *Launched on September 26, 1934, the* Queen Mary *made her maiden voyage on May 27, 1936. Some 30 years later, on October 31, 1967, she started her final journey—the 516th—to Long Beach, where she has remained since.* © Bill Ross/CORBIS

LEFT: *It could be Italy . . . a gondola in Naples—there are about a mile's worth of canals in Naples, CA, the large semi-circular Rivo Alto Canal and shorter Naples Canal.* © Richard Cummins/CORBIS

LOS ANGELES

Location 34.052°N 118.242°W
Area 469.1 square miles
Altitude 330 feet above sea level
City Population 3,694,820
Time Zone Pacific Daylight Saving

The largest city in California and second largest in the United States, Los Angeles was originally founded in 1781 by Franciscan missionaries as part of New Spain and given the name El Pueblo de Nuestra Senora la Reina de los Angeles de Porciuncula (the town of Our Lady, Queen of the Angels at the Little Portion). Mexico achieved independence from Spain in 1821 and in 1845 was named capital of Mexican California, but the following year a group raised the California Bear flag and declared independence from Mexico. U.S. troops quickly took control of other towns and cities in California, such as Monterey and San Francisco, although the full conquest of Los Angeles took some considerable time and effort before finally being achieved by Lieutenant Colonel John C. Fremont. Mexico and the United States then signed a Treaty of Capitulation on January 13, 1847.

Los Angeles was incorporated as a city in April 1850, but there were still numerous Mexican bandit raids on the city to contend with. Juan Flores threatened a full-scale invasion in 1856, while Tiburcio Vasquez was finally apprehended in 1874; both men went to the gallows.

In 1876 the Southern Pacific Railroad arrived in Los Angeles and the city began to increase its size and importance relative to neighboring San Francisco, in whose shadow it had languished. The discovery of oil in the early 1890s and the subsequent creation of a proper port terminal, railway terminal and assorted industries within the city eventually enabled Los Angeles to become the most important city in the state of California.

By the turn of the century it began to attract an altogether new industry, with many of the pioneering film makers flocking to Los Angeles in general and Hollywood, to the north-west of the city, in particular. While Hollywood is today something of generic term to describe all film-making activity in the city, many of the major film companies retain offices and studios within the area.

If the film industry has made Los Angeles famous, then there are countless other industries that made it rich. Its car industry was second only to Detroit, tire industry second only to Akron, and its garment-manufacturing and banking facilities made it a major rival to New York. While many of these industries have closed, newer industries have grown up in their place, with television and radio facilities in particular ensuring the city retains its position as the entertainment capital of the country.

FAR LEFT: *Palm trees in Downtown Los Angeles.*
© Stuart Westmorland/CORBIS

BELOW: *The classic view of Los Angeles at night.*
© Craig Aurness/CORBIS

Downtown Los Angeles is illuminated by the setting sun. The tallest building (central in photograph) is the 1989 U.S. Bank Tower (1,018ft); to its left is the 858ft Aon Center—the tallest building west of the Mississippi River from 1974 to 1982 until surpassed by JP Morgan Chase Tower in Houston. © Joseph Sohm; ChromoSohm Inc./CORBIS

ONE WILSHIRE

View toward Downtown Los Angeles and over MacArthur Park. Originally called Westlake Park, MacArthur Park was laid out in the 1880s. It occupies 32 acres. Wilshire Boulevard formerly went around the park, but by 1934 it sliced right through the middle. The name was changed to General Douglas MacArthur Park at the conclusion of World War II. © Bill Varie/CORBIS

RIGHT: *Rush-hour traffic on a Los Angeles highway—the city is known for freeway gridlock of legendary proportions.* © D. Boone/CORBIS

FAR RIGHT: *Los Angeles skyline at dusk.* © Joseph Sohm; Visions of America/CORBIS

MEMPHIS

Location 35.149°N 90.048°W
Area 279.3 square miles
Altitude 254 feet above sea level
City Population 650,100
Time Zone Central

The city and port of Memphis is situated above the Mississippi River and got its name from the similarities of its riverside position with the ancient Egyptian city of Memphis. Initially settled by the Chickasaw tribe, the city was believed to have been visited by Spanish explorer Hernando de Soto before French settlers built Fort Prudhomme in its vicinity.

Founded in 1819 and incorporated as a city in 1826, it was the scene of a major Civil War battle when Union forces captured Memphis from the Confederates in 1862. Over the next hundred or so years the city became an important trade and industrial center, with cotton, timber, and livestock markets competing with the manufacturing of textiles and chemicals. Memphis is also famed for its thriving musical scene, most notably blues music and rock and roll. It was home to the legendary soul and R&B label Stax and, most especially, Elvis Presley, who moved to the city with his family in 1948.

It was Presley's visit to the Memphis Recording Service to record two songs as a present to his mother that alerted Sun Records' boss Sam Phillips to his talents, and his subsequent recording of *That's All Right Mama* is usually regarded as the start of the rock and roll era. The presence of Elvis' Graceland home has made the city something of a pilgrim destination ever since Presley's death in 1977, the resulting tourism trade making a considerable contribution to the city's growing wealth.

The city suffered a yellow fever epidemic in 1870 which greatly reduced the population; it has remained fairly constant over the last two decades—646,000 in 1980 had risen to only 650,000 by 2000. It is, however, the largest city in Tennessee and the county seat of Shelby County.

RIGHT: *Flowers surround Elvis Presley's gravestone in the Meditation Gardens area of Graceland during Elvis Week. Huge numbers of fans attended the 25th anniversary of Presley's August 16, 1977, death. Graceland is the second-most visited home in America behind the White House.* © Mario Tama/Getty Images

FAR RIGHT: *Pedestrians wander down club-lined Beale Street in Memphis at sunset. The Blues, it is said, were born on Beale Street, and it was the home to famous blues musicians such as W.C. Handy who wrote the first blues song here in 1909. In addition to the musical heritage, the street shows other signs of its history—at A. Schwabs, a dry-goods store over 100 years old—browsers can shop for bargains.* © Kevin Fleming/CORBIS

BLUES
HALL
JUKE JOINT
Have a
Coke
Coca-Cola
THIS
IS
IT!
Restaurant
JAZZ Lounge

LEFT: *The original Peabody Hotel was founded in 1869. Today's hotel was opened in 1925 but fell into disrepair. It was revived on July 31, 1975, when Jack Belz bought it for $75,000 and began a $24-million renovation. The hotel reopened in 1981, 56 years after its original grand opening (1925). Restored to its late 19th-century elegance, the Peabody is in the heart of Memphis, two blocks from Beale Street. It is famous for its trained ducks, who live in the Duck Palace on the roof. Every day at 11:00 a.m. they troop into the elevator and ride down to the lobby, where they march into the fountain. At 5:00 p.m. they march back to the elevator and return to their palace.* © Kevin Fleming/CORBIS

BELOW: *The sun sets over a Mississippi paddleboat and the Memphis Business Journal Building.* © Kevin Fleming/CORBIS

MIAMI

Location 25.773°N 80.193°W
Area 35.7 square miles
Altitude 11 feet above sea level
City Population 362,470
Time Zone Eastern

Despite its relative youth, Miami, situated on the southern tip of the Florida peninsula, is a magnet for tourism, business, immigrants, and the recently retired. Little wonder the area is one of the most varied you'll find. The seaport is a regular stop on the cruise circuit, while the airport rivals New York in popularity. The proximity of not one but two national parks, the Biscayne and Everglades, means tourists who arrive are spoiled for leisure destinations.

The history of Miami, the second largest city in the state of Florida, dates from the arrival in the late 19th century of the railroad: prior to this, few had considered the outpost worth visiting. Miami Beach, a favored middle-class vacation haunt, was developed in 1912 by a millionaire named Carl Fisher. Others developed different areas in their desired image and, with winter visitors putting pressure on accommodation, Miami burgeoned in population from 30,000 to 100,000 in five years (the current population approaches 400,000). The culturally diverse population includes many Cubans and Haitians who have made the city their home. The 1990 census revealed nearly 50 percent of the city population was Hispanic, and predominantly of Cuban descent.

Architecturally, Miami has outstanding landmarks in the likes of the Sun Trust Building whose lighting changes to reflect the seasons, and the 55-story Southeast Financial Center. And, given that the *Miami Vice* TV series focused on law and order, it's appropriate that the city boasts the American Police Hall of Fame and Museum, honoring fallen lawmen across the nation. Sports-wise, the Miami Dolphins and Florida Marlins are prominent football and baseball teams, while college football's Orange Bowl final is played here.

Last but far from least, Miami's Florida International University is home to the National Hurricane Center while the headquarters of the U.S. Armed Forces Southern Command, responsible for military operations in Central and South America, is also in the city.

RIGHT: *Miami's World Trade Center at 777 NW 72 Avenue is one of 300 centers located in 91 countries with a total membership of 2 million corporate members and associates—the pre-eminent global trade organization. Also visible is Miami's Metromover system—a free, automated, electrically powered, fully automated people-mover system that serves downtown Miami from Omni to Brickell. The original system opened on April 17, 1986; the Omni/Brickell extensions on May 26, 1994. In 2003 6,798,887 people used it.*
© B.S.P.I./CORBIS

A century ago Miami was a mosquito-ridden swamp. Today it is an exciting vibrant city and Miami Beach, a long arm of land between the ocean and the mainland, is a fabulous place full of Art Deco buildings particularly along Ocean Drive.
© Robert Landau/CORBIS

Miami skyline. Over the years Miami has become increasingly high-rise: today, of its 20 tallest buildings, six have been built in the 21st century including the tallest, the Four Seasons Tower and Hotel which is 789ft tall with 64 floors. In Miami Beach the same is true but more so. The 15 tallest buildings were built in the last decade: seven of the top ten this century. © Joseph Sohm; Visions of America/CORBIS

INSET: *A bicyclist rides past an eight-foot fiberglass flamingo in South Beach, Florida. This was part of a 2002 nationwide public art project. Miami got fiberglass flamingos; Cincinnati pigs; there were fish in New Orleans, and cows in New York and Chicago.* © Joe Raedle/Getty Images

SunBank

MILWAUKEE

Location 43.038°N 87.906°W
Area 96.1 square miles
Altitude 634 feet above sea level
City Population 596,974
Time Zone Central

Located on Lake Michigan, Milwaukee is the largest city within the state of Wisconsin, with nearly 600,000 inhabitants within the city and over 1.5 million in the local metropolitan area. The area was believed to have been first inhabited by various Indian tribes such as the Fox, Mascouten, Potawatomi and Winnebago and derived its name from the Indian word *Millioke*, which either meant "The Good Land" or "gathering place by the water." French missionaries and traders passed through the area in the 17th and 18th centuries and the city soon became an important fur-trading point, closely followed by land speculators from the eastern seaboard. Frenchman Solomon Juneau settled in the area in 1818 and founded a town on the east side of the Milwaukee River in 1833; by 1846 the town had grown so much that it subsequently incorporated neighboring towns Kilbourn and Walker's Point and became a city, with Juneau serving as the first mayor. A statue of Solomon Juneau is to be found within the city, looking over the downtown buildings with its back to Lake Michigan.

Later the same decade came an influx of German immigrants, and Milwaukee retains a large German-American population. They were also followed by Irish, Scandinavians, Poles, Czechs, and Italians, and with them came their politics—for many years Milwaukee was considered a socialist city! The first socialist mayor, Emil Seidel who was elected in 1910, made one of his first priorities the creation of a Child Welfare Commission—child mortality fell and the average life expectancy of the Milwaukeean almost doubled.

A major shipping center, the city is also a leading producer of electrical equipment, heavy machinery, and diesel and petrol engines. The city's population has actually fallen over the last 20 years as nearly 50,000 migrated to the metropolitan area rather than live within the city itself.

RIGHT: *Bikers cruise Water Street in Downtown Milwaukee on August 28, 2003. More than 250,000 Harley-Davidson enthusiasts converged on the area to celebrate the company's 100th anniversary.* © Scott Olson/Getty Images

FAR RIGHT: *Milwaukee's Third Ward District along Lake Michigan. Next to Downtown, it is bordered by highway I-194 to the north, the Milwaukee River to the south and west, and Lake Michigan to the east. It is a fashionable area today, a hub for artistic activity and exhibitions, and home to galleries and theaters.* © Richard Cummins/CORBIS

bank

LEFT: *Milwaukee and the Menomonie River. At right, the city's tallest building, the 1973 U.S. Bank Center (601ft), whose structural engineer was Fazlur Khan, who also worked on the John Hancock Center and Sears Tower. In the center of the photograph is the 549ft Faison Building at 100 East Wisconsin with its intricate roof that harks back to old German vernacular architecture. At left is the peaked tower of the Milwaukee Center (426ft). In the foreground is the new Sixth Street Viaduct across the Menomonee River Valley which opened in early September 2002.* © Joseph Sohm; Visions of America/CORBIS

MINNEAPOLIS

Location 44.98°N 93.263°W
Area 54.9 square miles
Altitude 815 feet above sea level
City Population 382,618
Time Zone Central

Taking its name from the Dakota word for water (*minne*) and the Greek word for city (*polis*), Minneapolis is the largest city in Minnesota and stands on the Mississippi River, across from the state capital of St. Paul—the two are known as The Twin Cities.

The city of Minneapolis grew up around the Saint Anthony Falls, the only waterfall to be found on the Mississippi River and what was once the end of the navigational section of the river. It is believed that Father Louis Hennepin was the first European to explore the area extensively (the local county is known as Hennepin County) and the building of Fort Snelling in the area soon led to villages and towns springing up close by. Despite the protection afforded by the fort, settlers were prohibited to stay on land nearby without special permission, with the result that most of the settlements grew up on the northeast side of the river. In 1852 President Fillmore reduced the amount of land controlled by the fort and settlements soon sprung up on the southwest bank, including the village of Minneapolis. It became a city in 1867 and merged with nearby Saint Anthony five years later.

At first the city grew in relation to the river, maximizing the amount of land that could be used by building parallel to the river, before eventually turning outward. While the city was initially an important center for the lumber industry, it soon became "the milling capital of the world" as the processing of grain from the Great Plains took control and is still known today in many quarters as "Mill City." Major employers in the city include General Mills and Pillsbury, two of the main milling companies, while it is also home to thriving medical and financial industries and what is claimed to be the largest shopping mall in the United States, the Mall of America.

RIGHT: *Skywalk and skyscrapers in Minneapolis. The unmistakable Foshay Tower was built in 1929, its design inspired by the Washington Monument in Washington, DC. At 447ft the tallest building in Minneapolis from 1929 to 1971, it was inducted into the National Register of Historic Places in 1977. The 'FOSHAY' letters are 10ft high.* © Wes Thompson/CORBIS

FAR RIGHT: *Downtown Minneapolis. The tallest building, in the center of the photograph, is the 776ft 225 South Sixth built in 1992. The chief architect was James Ingo Freed and the building was designed as the headquarters of First Bank, now U.S. Bancorp. The building changed its name to 225 South Sixth in 2002. To its right is the Cesar Pelli-designed Wells Fargo Center (originally the Norwest Tower). Built in 1988 and 773ft tall, it received the Urban Land Institute's Award for Excellence in Large Scale Office Development in 1989.*
© Joseph Sohm; ChromoSohm Inc./CORBIS

FOSHAY
the old spaghetti factory

RIGHT: *The Frederick R. Weisman Art Museum was built in 1993 to the design of Frank O. Gehry. It is located on the Minneapolis campus of the University of Minnesota, on the east bank of the Mississippi River. Founded in 1934, the museum's reflective stainless-steel exterior is a modern casing for a collection that concentrates on early 20th century American artists such as Georgia O'Keeffe and Marsden Hartley, as well as a diverse selection of contemporary art.* © Bill Ross/CORBIS

MOBILE

Location 30.694°N 88.043°W
Area 117.9 square miles
Altitude 16 feet above sea level
City Population 198,915
Time Zone Central

Taking its name from the Mobile (Mauvile or Maubila) Indians who inhabited the area at the time of founding, Mobile has a curent population of nearly 200,000. It has passed through several hands, beginning life as the capital of the French colony of Louisiana, and was transferred to the British in 1763 via the Treaty of Paris.

The Spanish captured Mobile in 1780 under Bernardo de Gálvez, aware of its important strategic position at the head of Mobile Bay and at the mouth of the Mobile River, and held it until it was captured by the American General Wilkinson in 1814; by then it was the second largest seaport on the Gulf Coast. It is also the only seaport in Alabama and the second largest city in the state.

Mobile was a major American Civil War outpost, and was heavily fortified by the Confederates. Union naval forces under Admiral David Farragut won the Battle of Mobile Bay, but in May 1865 an ammunition depot explosion killed 300 people. After the war the harbor was improved and deepened, and shipbuilding flourished. The Tennessee–Tombigbee waterway, completed in 1984, provided access to the Gulf of Mexico by connecting North Mississippi's Tennessee River with the Tombigbee River in West Alabama. This helped Mobile enjoy a period of business growth and redevelopment, and current industrial success stories include oil, paper, textiles, aluminum, and chemicals.

Notable yearly activities that take place in Mobile include the Senior Bowl, Azalea Trail Festival (dating from 1929), Mardi Gras (the oldest in the country), and the Junior Miss Pageant, while the many historical events associated with the Civil War are remembered via the homes of Admiral Raphael Semmes and General Braxton Bragg, the headquarters of General Canby, and Forts Morgan and Gaines at the entrance to Mobile Bay.

RIGHT: *Floral landscape at Bellingrath Home, just outside Mobile in Theodore. The original 60 acres were purchased by Walter Bellingrath, the originator of Mobile's Coca-Cola bottling operation, in 1917. A 1927 European trip saw the Bellingraths concentrate on the gardens and build a new house (completed in 1935) designed by George B. Rogers. Mobile and its environs are known for their colorful azaleas, camellias, and cornuses.* © Raymond Gehman/CORBIS

ABOVE: *The Gulf of Mexico can suffer from extreme weather. This is the result of Cyclone George in 1998.* © Mobile Press Register/Corbis Sygma

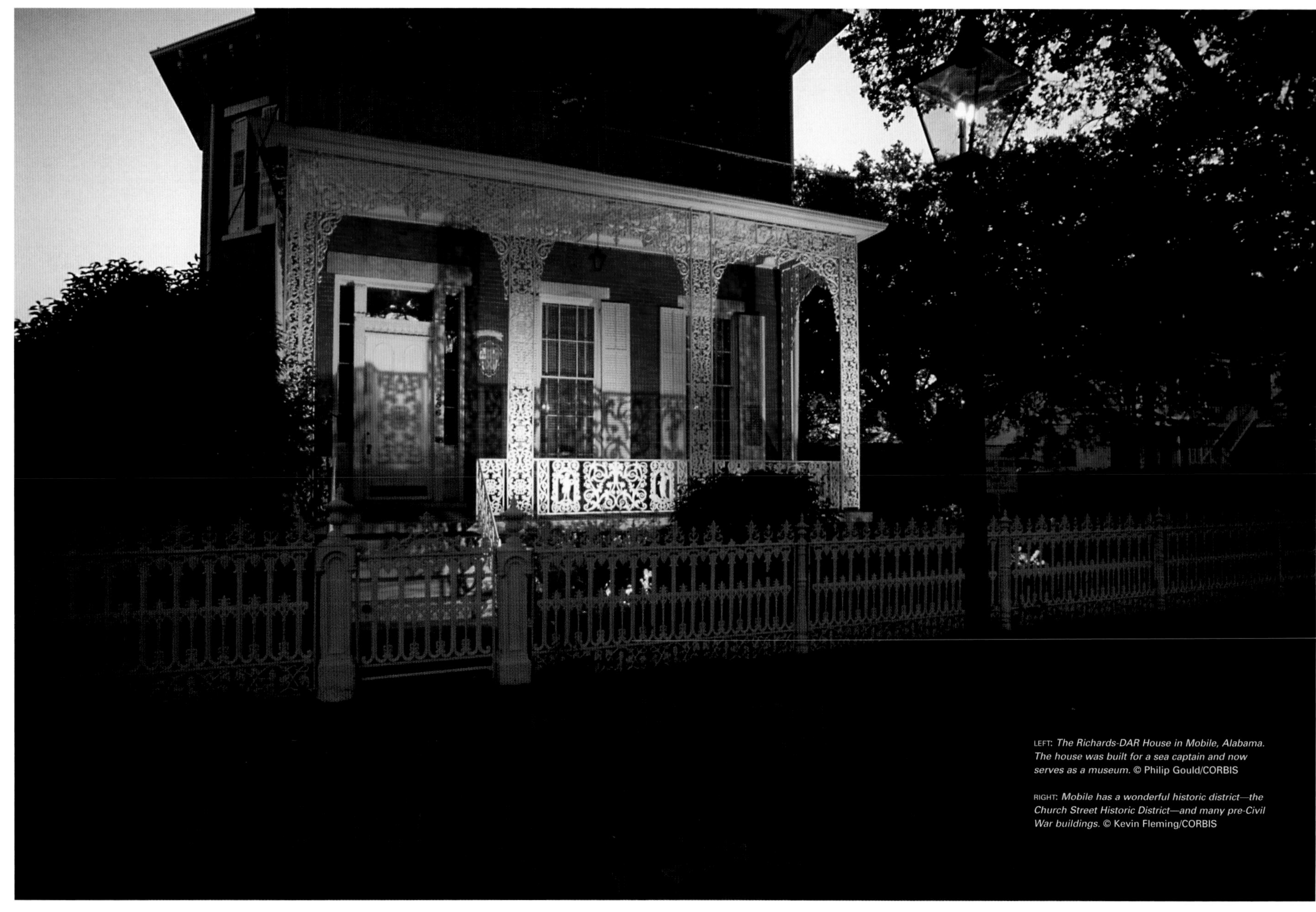

LEFT: *The Richards-DAR House in Mobile, Alabama. The house was built for a sea captain and now serves as a museum.* © Philip Gould/CORBIS

RIGHT: *Mobile has a wonderful historic district—the Church Street Historic District—and many pre-Civil War buildings.* © Kevin Fleming/CORBIS

NASHVILLE

Location 36.165°N 86.784°W
Area 4.6 square miles
Altitude 383 feet above sea level
City Population 4,878,000
Time Zone Central

Nashville was founded as Fort Nashborough in 1779, named in honor of acclaimed Revolutionary War hero General Francis Nash. This makes it older than both the state of Tennessee and the U.S. Constitution. French fur traders had earlier established a trading post around 1717, but Englishman James Robertson (who is buried there) built a log stockade in 1779 by the banks of the Cumberland River. Five years later the community's name changed to Nashville.

Nashville became the state capital of Tennessee in 1812, this being confirmed in 1843 after Knoxville and Murfreesboro had set their caps at that status. A new capitol building was started in 1845 but not finished until 1859, but its Greek-inspired architecture dominated the city skyline until dwarfed by the high-rise constructions of the mid-20th century.

Nashville's prosperity relied on the river and the railroad, with cotton an important commodity and the city was occupied by Federal troops in 1862 under D. C. Buell. It became an important Union stronghold for the remainder of the Civil War, and Union General G. H. Thomas won a decisive victory over J. B. Hood in the Battle of Nashville in December 1864, one of the last major battles of the Civil War. With peace, Nashville once again experienced a growth in population, business, industry, and education.

Nashville has many buildings of classical design, including a replica of the Parthenon, built in 1897, and has earned the nickname "the Athens of the South."

Country music claims Nashville as its capital, and it is known as "Music City, USA." The Grand Ole Opry concert venue/radio show was established in 1925, and the city now boasts Music Row, where the record company offices and studios are congregated, the Country Music Hall of Fame and museum and a number of showcase venues like the Bluebird Cafe where stars old, and new can perform.

BELOW: *Street furniture gone mad: a "Music City" street lined with advertising signs.* © Joel W. Rogers/CORBIS

RIGHT: *The Nashville skyline is dominated by the BellSouth Building built in 1994. At 617ft, the tallest building in Tennessee is nicknamed the "Batman Building," because of its two "ears."* © Jeff Vanuga/CORBIS

LIVE 95

FAR LEFT: *The Country Music Hall of Fame.* © Mark E. Gibson/ CORBIS

LEFT: *Nashville has been the capital of country music since the 1930s. This is the 2004 version: Darryl Worley at the CMA Music Festival.* © Getty Images

NEW ORLEANS

Location 29.954°N 90.075°W
Area 180.6 square miles
Altitude 11 feet above sea level
City Population 484,674
Time Zone : Central

New Orleans gains its nickname of "the Crescent City" from its position on a bend of the Mississippi River, about 107 miles from the Gulf of Mexico and with Lake Pontchartrain on its other side. It is the largest city in Louisiana and one of the largest in the south. Its status as a port helped make it a leading industrial center, while petrochemical plants spread along the Mississippi to the west.

The French influence has been all-pervading since it was founded in 1718 by explorers Iberville and Bienville, who named the city Nouvelle Orleans after the Duke of Orleans. Louisiana was transferred to Spain in 1762 before briefly returning to France and then becoming part of the U.S. in 1803. Many flags have flown over the city, which was incorporated in 1805, each experience adding to the rich cultural mix.

During the 1850s, yellow fever attacked the city's population, many of whom fled the city; it wasn't until the end of the century when the swamps were drained and New Orleans given a proper sewerage system that the climate began to improve. The Civil War saw New Orleans, the largest city of the Confederacy, fall in 1862 to Admiral David G. Farragut and suffer a gruelling 15-year spell under Union occupation when prosperity suffered.

In 1969 Hurricane Camille swept through the region, resulting in deaths and property damage. 1978 saw the historic election of African-American mayor Ernest "Dutch" Morial, the city experiencing economic growth under his leadership. Tourism boomed, annual visitor numbers exceeding six million, while a World's Fair in 1984 saw the city's riverfront acquire shopping malls and condominiums. On the minus side, falling petroleum prices saw oil companies moving to Houston to cut costs.

Tourist attractions in New Orleans are many and various, and include Jackson Square, the Cabildo (formerly the government building) and St. Louis Cathedral. The annual Mardi Gras is the best-known festival in the United States and combines music, for which the city is well known thanks to performers ranging from Fats Domino to Doctor John, with food, another speciality.

Also noteworthy is the Jazzland Theme Park, a few miles to the east, while Chalmette, site of the famous battle of New Orleans between British soldiers and General Andrew Jackson's militiamen, is part of the Jean Lafitte National Historical Park.

St. Louis Cathedral in Chartres Street was built in 1794 to the designs of Adrien de Pauger. Next door is the Cabildo, the Spanish seat of government in which the Louisiana Purchase was signed. In front of the cathedral is Jackson Square—and an equestrian statue of Andrew Jackson—where executions used to take place. No longer! Today's French Quarter, is the heart of New Orleans. © D. Boone/CORBIS

FAR RIGHT: *Downtown New Orleans at twilight. The tallest building in the city is the 1972-built One Shell Square (697ft), another design by Skidmore, Owings & Merrill. Smaller, at 481ft, (central, illuminated) is the 1987 LL&E Tower designed by Welton Becket Associates.* © Richard Cummins/CORBIS

OVERLEAF: *Lake Pontchartrain is known for its Causeway Bridge, at nearly 24 miles the world's longest overwater highway bridge, that carries I-10 over the lake. Lake Pontchartrain was named for the eponymous count, the Navy Minister of Louis XIV of France who is himself immortalized in the name Louisiana.* © Joseph Sohm/CORBIS

NEW YORK CITY

Location 40.714°N 74.006°W
Area 303.3 square miles
Altitude 6 feet above sea level
City Population 8,008,278
Time Zone Eastern

Affectionately known as "The Big Apple," New York City is the largest city in America and also lays claim to the title "capital of the world," a status no doubt reflected by the fact the United Nations headquarters are located within the city.

Although Indian tribes such as the Manhattoes and Canarsies inhabited the area for many hundreds of years, the first proper settlement of the area came with the arrival of the Dutch, who landed at what is now the southern tip of Manhattan in 1626 and called the town New Amsterdam. The British captured the town in 1664 and renamed it New York, after the Duke of York, and after further struggles between the Dutch and British, it was formally signed over to the British in the Treaty of Breda in 1667.

New York was in British hands when the War of Independence ended in 1783. Thereafter, rapid development and growth saw New York increase its importance and by 1835 it had overtaken Philadelphia as the largest city in the United States. The Civil War saw the city divided for, although based in the north and expected to favor the Union forces, its strong commercial ties with the south led to the Draft Riots of 1863, when upward of 50,000 protesters took to the streets in protest against President Abraham Lincoln's Enrolment Act of Conscription. After five days of rioting, a reported 1,200 were dead and extensive property damage had been caused in the worst civil unrest in American history.

After the war, New York and its famous skyline incorporating the Statue of Liberty became an important first stepping stone for millions of European immigrants arriving in the United States. While many headed inland, those who remained enabled New York to increase its population and stature; by 2000 the population had hit eight million and the city was home to some of the largest corporations in America. The city is also the financial capital of the world and home to Wall Street.

It is, of course, the events of September 11, 2001, that have brought New York City into sharp focus around the world; two hijacked planes crashed into the World Trade Center, bring both the North and South Towers crashing to the ground with the loss of more than 3,000 lives. A Freedom Tower is to be built on the site and is intended to be the largest skyscraper in the world, a perfect symbol of New York's defiance in the face of terrorism.

RIGHT: *America's figurehead—visitors in the Statue of Liberty's Crown.* © Bettmann/CORBIS

FAR RIGHT: *Aerial view of Central Park. Opened in 1876, it is still an oasis amongst the high-rises.* © David Ball/CORBIS

Tourists view the Statue of Liberty from a Circle Line Boat in New York Harbor. The 306ft 8in statue was designed by French sculptor Frederic-Auguste Bartholdi and declared the Statue of Liberty National Monument in 1924. © Joseph Sohm; ChromoSohm Inc./CORBIS

The Empire State Building dominates any view of Manhattan—at 1,472ft, with 102 stories, following the tragedy of 9/11, it is once more the tallest building in New York City. © David Sailors/CORBIS

RIGHT: *Frank Lloyd Wright's Solomon R. Guggenheim Museum was opened in 1959: the building is still more visited than its exhibitions.* © Jerry Arcieri/CORBIS

OVERLEAF: *Everyone's image of New York—taxi traffic in Times Square.* © Joseph Sohm; Visions of America/CORBIS

ONE WAY
MUSEUM
SOLOMON R GUGGENHEIM MUSEUM
ICE CREAM

MR. PEANUT
Relax. Go Nuts.
BREAKFAST-DINNER
AFTER THEATRE SNACKS
SUNTORY WHISKY
Coca-Cola
INDULGE YOURSELF! HAVE A DIET COKE!
HAUNTING
maxell
NOVOTEL

Mountain Dew
PLAY
ALL STAR CAFE
CROSSWORDS
AND WIN
Sports Illustrated
ALL STAR
THE GAME BEGINS HERE
Theatre
Stage Right
the LION in WINTER
The Mineola Twins
Roundabout Theatre Company
OFFICIAL ALL STAR
POLICE LINE DO NOT CROSS
4Y53
458-MHB

OKLAHOMA CITY

Location 35.467°N 97.516°W
Area 625 square miles
Altitude 1,195 feet above sea level
City Population 506,132
Time Zone Central

Oklahoma City is the capital and largest city of the state with which it shares its name. Its total metropolitan population represents a third of the entire state's population and it is 29th largest city in the United States.

Cotton, wheat, and livestock have been staples of Oklahoma's economy, but the most important of all natural resources is oil. The first well was drilled in 1888, and Oklahoma City became one of the most important natural gas and petroleum centers of the world. Oil and gas have declined somewhat in importance today, however. Many of Oklahoma's factories process local foods and minerals, but its chief manufactures include non-electrical machinery and fabricated metal products. Military bases and other government facilities are also important.

Oklahoma experienced a boom during the 1970s when oil prices rose dramatically. In the mid-1980s, however, its economy was hurt (as it had been in the 1930s) by over-dependence on a single industry, as oil prices fell rapidly.

The downtown Bricktown entertainment district, developed in the past decade, is one of the city's most popular destinations. The historic area is full of restaurants, clubs, music venues, and shops. With the largest Asian population in the state, Oklahoma City also boasts varied cultures and cuisine.

The Crystal Bridge rivals Oklahoma's skyscrapers as visual attractions. Designed by I. M. Pei with the Tivoli Gardens in Copenhagen as his inspiration, the Crystal Bridge is in fact a tropical conservatory at the Myriad Botanical Gardens. Sports fans are well catered for, and Remington Park in the northeast of the city is the state's largest race-track.

Sadly, Oklahoma hit the headlines on April 19, 1995, when Timothy McVeigh and accomplices bombed the Murrah Federal Building, killing 168 in the worst terrorist attack on American soil until the 9/11 attacks on New York and Washington.

RIGHT: *The Oklahoma City skyline is dominated by the 500ft Bank One Tower, built in 1971. Just to its left in this photograph is the spire of the First National Center (446ft) built in 1931.* © CORBIS

FAR RIGHT: *Statue below the Alfred P. Murrah Federal Building, the site of the Oklahoma City bombing on April 19, 1995, in which 168 men, women, and children lost their lives. The site is now part of the Oklahoma City National Memorial.* © Dave G. Houser/CORBIS

RIGHT: *Gate and Reflecting Pool at the Oklahoma City National Memorial. They stand on the site of the terrorist bombing of the Alfred Murrah Federal Building, marking the moment of destruction.*
© Jeff Albertson/CORBIS

PHILADELPHIA

Location 39.952°N 75.164°W
Area 135.1 square miles
Altitude 40 feet above sea level
City Population 1,517,550
Time Zone Eastern

Founded by William Penn in 1862, Philadelphia was the original capital of the United States from 1790 until 1800. For many years "Philly" has been primarily an industrial city as well as an important port on the Delaware River. The Declaration of Independence was signed here and the Liberty Bell still hangs in the city. It is also home to the U.S. Mint and inventor/statesman Benjamin Franklin is buried here. Independence Park is an L-shaped area west of the Delaware River that features Philadelphia's most renowned historical sites. Called the birthplace of American government, Independence Hall was built between 1732 and 1756 as Pennsylvania Statehouse, the colony's headquarters.

One of the country's best examples of Georgian architecture, its simple, understated lines also show the Quaker influence of Philadelphia's early days. The Assembly Room is where the delegates from the 13 colonies met to approve the Declaration of Independence on July 4, 1776; where the design of the U.S. flag was agreed upon in 1777; where the Articles of the Confederation were drafted in 1781; and where the Constitutional Convention was held in 1787, producing the U.S. Constitution.

Every New Year's Day sees the Mummers Parade when 30,000 men wearing sequins, feathers, makeup and risqué costumes spectacularly strut their way around town accompanied by accordions and glockenspiels. The Penn Relays, held at the University of Pennsylvania in April, is one of the world's oldest, largest, and best amateur athletic carnivals, while the Jambalaya Jam in May is a three-day celebration of Creole and Cajun food and New Orleans music.

RIGHT: *Schuylkill River and Philadelphia skyline. From left to right: Bell Atlantic Tower (739ft) built in 1991; the pyramid-topped Mellon Bank Center (792ft) was built in 1990; just visible Two Liberty Place (848ft) built in 1990; Independence Blue Cross Tower (625ft) also built in 1990; and the two identical towers of One and Two Commerce Square (565ft)—the first built in 1987, the second in 1992.* © Richard Cummins/CORBIS

ABOVE: *Members of the Broomall String Band perform as they march up Broad Street during the 103rd New Year's Day Mummer's Parade January 1, 2004 in Philadelphia, Pennsylvania. The day-long parade features four divisions of Comics, Fancy Clubs, Fancy Brigades, and String Bands. The clubs develop a theme, create costumes, build sets and props, and choreograph musical and dance numbers while competing for cash prizes.* © William Thomas Cain/Getty Images

OVERLEAF: *This view of Philadelphia shows, in the center, the two tallest buildings in the city: Two Liberty Place (left) and One Liberty Place. The tallest building in the city, One Liberty Place, at 945ft, was the first building in Philadelphia to break the gentlemen's agreement not to exceed the height of the William Penn statue on City Hall, which is on the left of the photograph. The right-hand skyscraper is the Mellon Bank Center.* © Richard Berenholtz/CORBIS

PNB PNB

PNCBANK

PHOENIX

Location 33.448°N 112.073°W
Area 474.9 square miles
Altitude 1,072 feet above sea level
City Population 1,321,045
Time Zone Mountain Standard

Phoenix was the brainchild of Jack Swilling, a former soldier whose vision of irrigating the Salt River Valley in 1868 created farmland. (The opening of the federally financed Roosevelt Dam in 1911 further transformed Arizona's once arid valleys.) The city got its name because it was a new town rising from the ruins of an old civilization, in this case the site of ancient Native American canals.

By 1880 Phoenix had a population of 2,500, and the next decade saw the foundations of the modern city laid. In 1886, one of the first electric plants in the west was installed, while a streetcar system and railroad link followed the next year. The tempo of economic life increased considerably as a result. In 1926, Phoenix's railroad links crossed the continent, and tourists from the east arrived to stay in dude ranches or enjoy a dry desert climate said to cure respiratory ailments.

Defense industries established during the war (when no fewer than three airfields were opened) continued to develop afterward. Manufacturing eventually overtook mining and agriculture in importance as service veterans who had been stationed in Phoenix made it their home and manufacturing moved there to utilize their labor.

The 1970s and 1980s saw many more high-technology industries arrive, while the diversion of Colorado River water to the city after 1968 and improved air-conditioning systems helped population grow exponentially, which in turn gave real estate and construction industries a boost: Phoenix is known as one of the west's latter-day boom towns. Phoenix's population recently nudged into seven figures, with the inclusion of the suburbs of Mesa, Scottsdale, Tempe, and Glendale.

Phoenix celebrates its origins with a number of Native American communities and reservations, including the Arizona Museum, Heard Museum, Phoenix Art Museum, and the Pueblo Grande Museum, whose excavations of Native American ruins are some 800 years old.

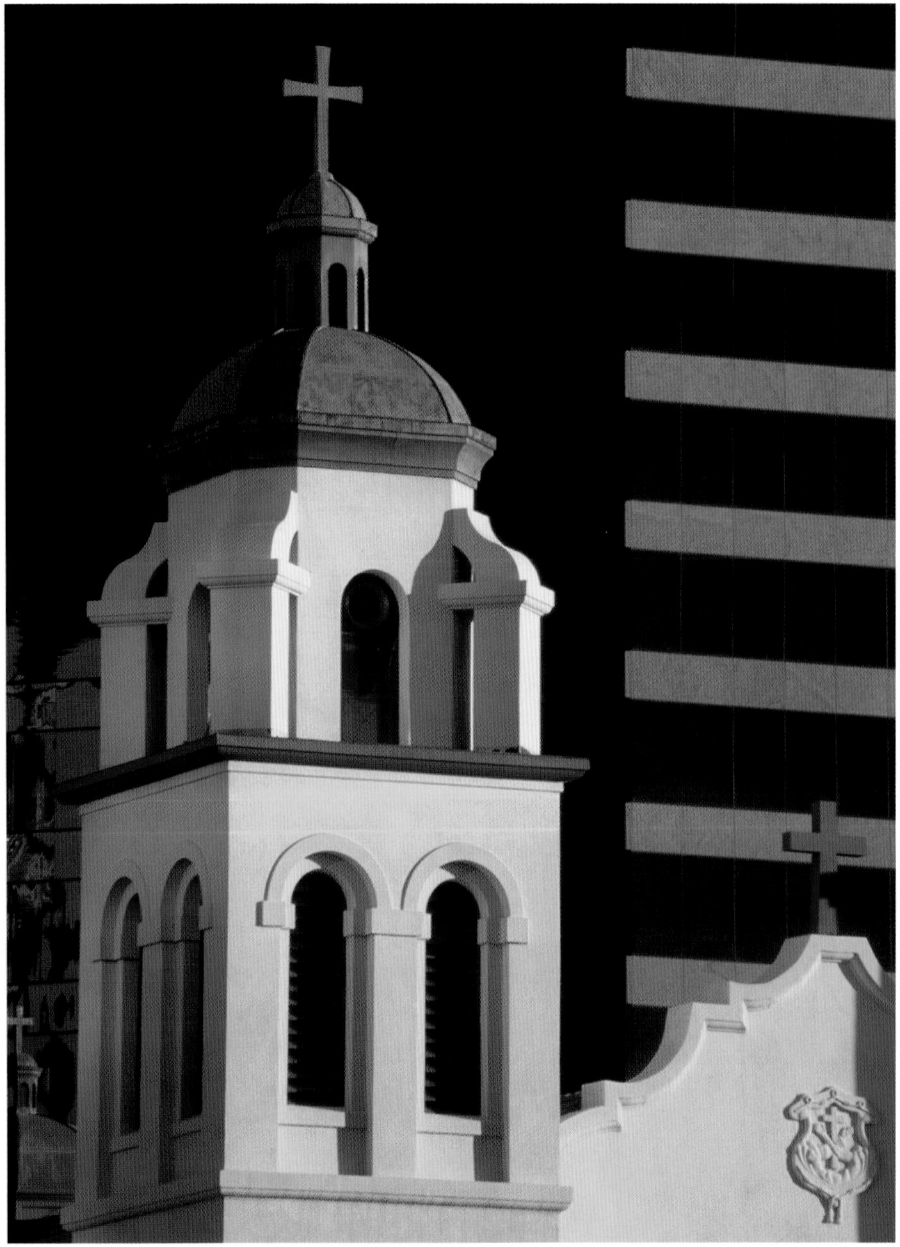

RIGHT: *Tower of Saint Mary's Basilica, founded in 1881 and staffed by the Franciscan Friars since 1895. The church was completed in 1914, became a national historical monument in 1978, and was designated a basilica in 1985 by Pope John Paul II, who visited Phoenix in 1987.* © Richard Cummins/CORBIS

FAR RIGHT: *Patriot Square Park.* © D. Boone/CORBIS

OVERLEAF: *Clouds cast shadows over Phoenix.* © Gerald French/CORBIS

PITTSBURGH

Location 40.440°N 79.996°W
Area 55.6 square miles
Altitude 770 feet above sea level
City Population 334,563
Time Zone Eastern

Incorporated in 1816, the seat of Allegheny County in southwest Pennsylvania is situated at the fork of the Allegheny and Monongahela rivers where they combine to form the Ohio River. Its position was ideal for the transportation in and out of raw materials, and this led to its position as "Steel City." Since the mid-1970s' slump in the steel industry, however, the city has moved to welcome service industries and, in the 1990s, technology-based companies.

Pittsburgh was founded near the Native American town of Shannopin, a late-17th-century fur-trading post. The French built Fort Duquesne on the site in the middle of the 18th century and this in turn became Fort Pitt when it fell to the English in 1758. (The blockhouse of Fort Pitt is now preserved in Point State Park.) The French had guarded the Ohio River which connected their colonies in Canada to their colonies in Louisiana, while the English wanted to expand their colonial power beyond the Appalachian Mountains. The site of Pittsburgh was, therefore, of considerable strategic importance.

A village was settled in 1760, and it prospered with the opening of the Northwest Territory; by 1790 Pittsburgh began to develop. It became known as the "Gateway to the West" during the 18th century and, as natural resources were discovered in the area, industry and commerce flourished. The 19th century saw printing shops, glassworks, and the iron industry find success.

Twentieth century Pittsburgh continues to innovate by creating clean, scenic areas such as Point State Park, while an office and hotel development, the Gateway Center, dominates a downtown area known as the Golden Triangle. Pittsburgh offers much in the way of culture, including a symphony orchestra, the Heinz Hall for the Performing Arts, the Carnegie Institute museums and Library, and the Andy Warhol Museum. It is also home to three major sports teams, the Pirates (baseball), Steelers (football), and Penguins (hockey).

BELOW LEFT: *From right to left: Steve Hegg of team Chevrolet/L.A. Sheriff, Eddy Gragus of team U.S. Postal Service and Fred Rodriguez of team Saturn race up Sycamore Street during the Thrift Drug Classic in Pittsburgh, Pennsylvania.* © Getty Images

RIGHT: *This classic view of the city shows the meeting of the Ohio, Monongahela, and Allegheny rvers. The bridge nearest the camera is the Fort Pitt Bridge over the Monongahela River which crosses over Point State Park to join the Fort Duquesne Bridge—the two names recording the French (in 1754) and British (in 1758) possession of the area. The topography of the city means that there are many bridges—one count reports over 2,000 bridges of 8 feet span or greater!* © Joseph Sohm; ChromoSohm Inc./CORBIS

Mellon
National City

Pittsburgh in the evening. The city's tallest building (to the right of center) is the U.S. Steel Tower (841ft) built in 1970; to its left, the castle-like One PPG Place, which has 231 glass spires, is 635ft tall, and was designed by Johnson/Burgee Architects. To its left is the 616ft Fifth Avenue Place, which is crowned by a pyramidal roof and a 178ft mast.
© Joseph Sohm; Visions of America/CORBIS

PORTLAND

Location 45.523°N 122.675°W
Area 134.3 square miles
Altitude 50 feet above sea level
City Population 529,121
Time Zone Pacific Daylight Saving

Portland, the largest conurbation in Oregon, was incorporated as a city in 1851. Settlers Asa Lovejoy and Francis Pettygrove had tossed a coin in 1845 to decide between naming the settlement Boston or Portland after their towns of origin: Pettygrove won.

The settlers were determined to build a community on the Willamette River near its junction with the Columbia where businesses could grow and prosper. By 1860 the population had swelled to nearly 3,000. Its growth was rapid thereafter as it served as a supply point for the California goldfields, and this was boosted further by the coming of the railroad (1883), the Alaska goldrush (1897–1900), and the Lewis & Clark Centennial Exposition (1905).

The Columbia River helped Portland become a business hub. It became an important deepwater port, with shipyards and international trade flourishing: British ships brought in supplies and left with furs in payment. The Hudson's Bay Company was particularly active around this time.

In 1875 a fire destroyed 20 blocks and nearly one-third of the business area of the city causing over a million dollars' damage. By 1900 the population exceeded 90,000. The current population approaches 500,000, but unlike many western U.S. cities, Portland has resisted the growth of urban sprawl by strictly limiting the metropolitan area and ring-fencing open space outside it.

Portland leads the country in light-rail development and boasts the best transit system in the country. An international airport and a U.S. Air Force base are nearby. Cultural needs are satisfied by a symphony orchestra and a ballet company, while the rose festival and the Pacific International Livestock Exposition and Rodeo are annual events. The area's natural beauty also attracts visitors, the Columbia River Gorge, Mt. Hood, and Mt. St. Helens just three nearby landmarks figuring on the tourist map.

RIGHT: *The 546ft Wells Fargo Center has been Portland's tallest building since 1972, but it is dwarfed by Mt Hood, tallest of Oregon's Cascade peaks at 11,239ft. The snow-clad summit of this dormant volcano is the most frequently climbed glaciated peak in North America..* © Steve Terrill/CORBIS

FAR RIGHT: *People strolling along the Willamette River in Tom McCall Waterfront Park.* © Dave G. Houser/CORBIS

OVERLEAF: *Skyline at dusk with the Oregon Convention Center in the foreground. The 500,000-square-foot convention center was built in 1990, designed by architect Robert J. Frasca.* © Thomas Wiewandt; Visions of America/CORBIS

NOW BOOKING
Conference
Portland Conference Center

RENO

Location 39.529°N 119.812°W
Area 69.1 square miles
Altitude 4,498 feet above sea level
City Population 180,480
Time Zone Pacific Daylight Saving

Reno is the county seat of Washoe County, Nevada. A 2000 census gave the city a population of 180,480, making it the second-largest conurbation in the state after Las Vegas. It lies 22 miles northeast of Lake Tahoe and is proud to be known as "The Biggest Little City in the World." It is famous for its casinos, and is the birthplace of the Harrah's gaming corporation.

Reno was first known as Fuller's Crossing, renamed after Charles Fuller who built a hotel and toll bridge across the Truckee River in 1860. He sold out to Myron C. Lake, who negotiated with the Central Pacific railroad to help build a town at "his" bridge, now Lake's Crossing. The railroad owners named the town after Jesse Lee Reno, an American army officer who had served in the Mexican War and was later killed in the Civil War. During this time, the rich Comstock Lode of silver was discovered and did much to help finance the Union's side in the Civil War.

Reno became a hotbed of gambling which never stopped even with Prohibition. Prostitution and bootleg liquor became big business under the guidance of such criminal masterminds as "Baby Face" Nelson, John Dillinger and "Pretty Boy" Floyd.

With the decline of the gold and silver boom and the start of the Depression, Mayor E. E. Roberts decided to license alcohol, gambling, and divorce, believing revenue could be gained. Thousands of married couples received a "quickie"divorce in Reno, where they only had to wait six weeks, and hotels and dude ranches were more than happy to accommodate them as they did so.

Bizarrely, weddings boomed during World War II, over 18,000 couples getting hitched in 1945 alone. The first commercial wedding chapel was established in 1956 next to the Washoe County Courthouse. For those with more cerebral ambitions, the city is home to the University of Nevada.

Many of Reno's old landmarks have been lost due to a rapid rate of expansion and rebuilding, but the city, whose current population approaches 200,000, remains prosperous. A decision to diversify away from reliance on gambling in the 1990s resulted in the building of the National Bowling Stadium, so more change may yet come.

RIGHT: *Colored spotlights illuminate casinos in Reno, Nevada, including the dome of the Silver Legacy. The 87,341-square-foot casino features 2,160 slots and 86 table games.*
© Mark E. Gibson/CORBIS

RIGHT AND OVERLEAF: *Casinos along Main Street, Reno. There are only three things to do in Reno, the guidebooks say: get married, get divorced . . . or really gamble.*
© Paul A. Souders/CORBIS

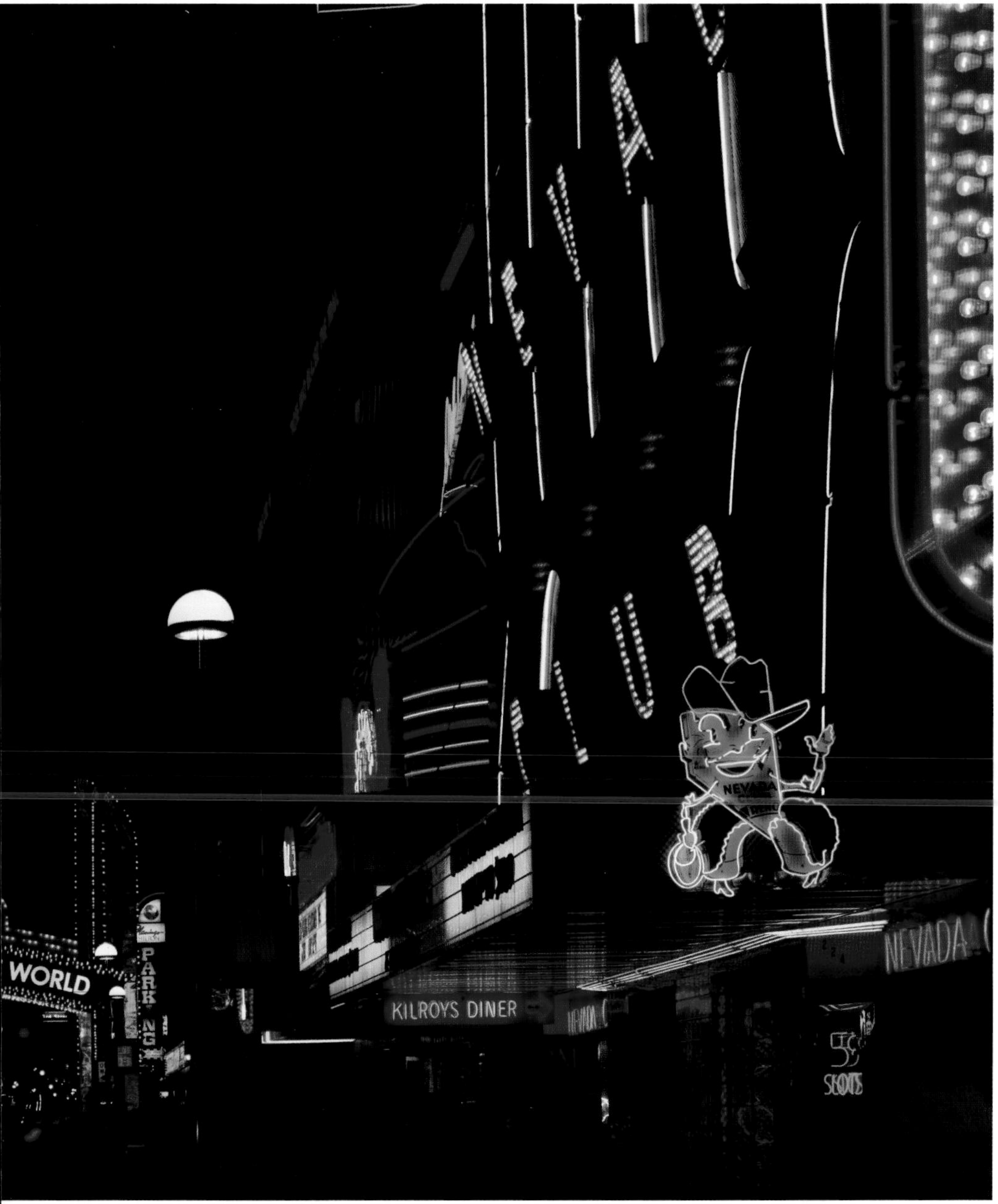
WORLD
KILROYS DINER
NEVADA

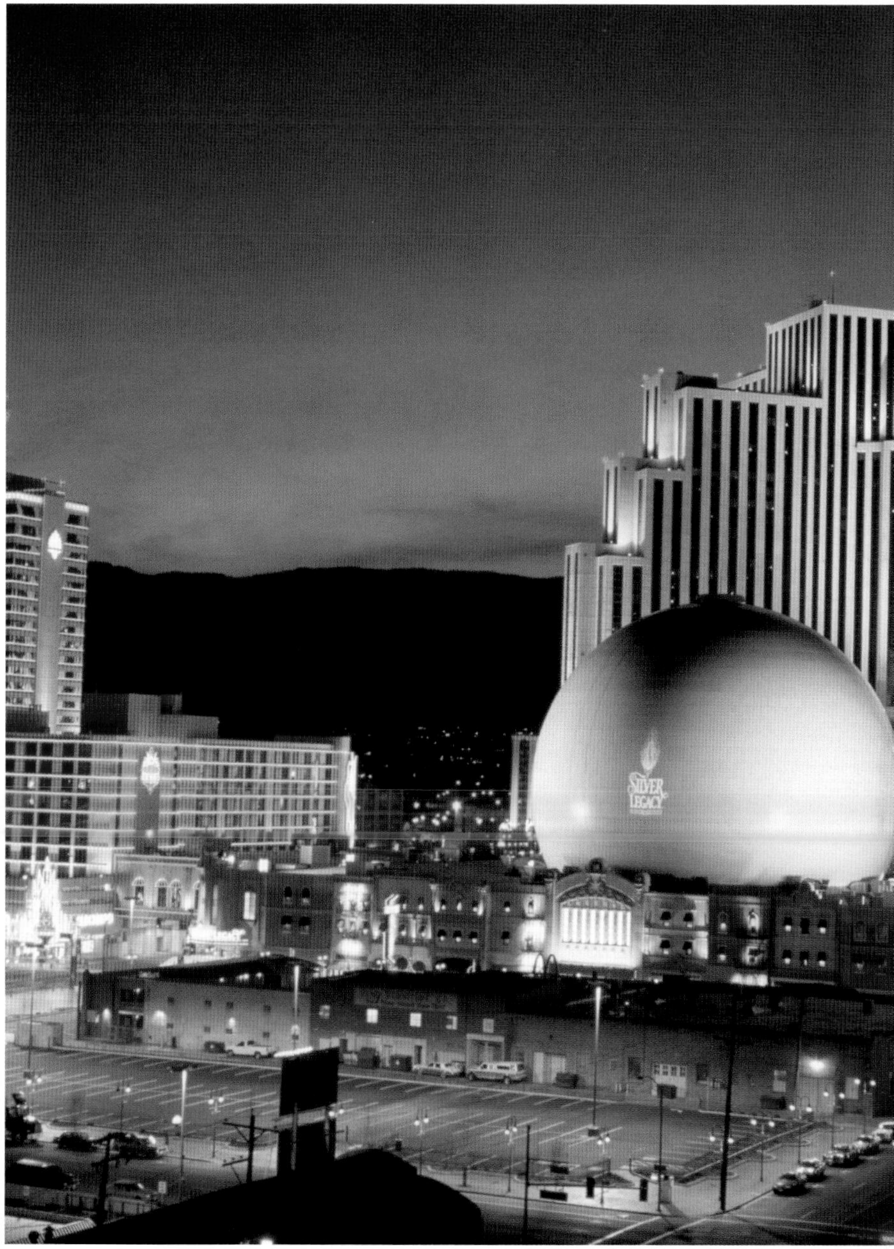
SILVER LEGACY

TEED WINNER
FOREST
ERICKS
& GRILLE
FLOOR
Fitzgeralds

RENO
BIGGEST LITTLE CITY IN THE WORLD
ONE WAY
Commercial Row
ONE WAY
3rd Street

SACRAMENTO

Location 38.581°N 121.493°W
Area 97.2 square miles
Altitude 20 feet above sea level
City Population 407,018
Time Zone Pacific Daylight Saving

The name of Sacramento, California, will forever be associated with the discovery of gold in 1848 at the junction of the American and Sacramento rivers, just 30 miles east of the city. News spread to all corners of the world and the result was the largest human migration in history. When California became a state two years later, it wasn't long before Sacramento, population 10,000, was confirmed as its capital.

But the city (founded by John A. Sutter in 1839 as a settlement called New Helvetia) had major problems with flooding, with devastation striking in 1850 and again in 1852. A third flood finally saw the city raised above the high-water mark.

The run-down city center was rebuilt in the mid-1960s, and with 53 historic buildings Old Sacramento boasts as many if not more historic buildings in its 28-acre area than any city in the west. The city annexed adjacent North Sacramento in 1965 and in the late 20th century was one of the fastest-growing U.S. conurbations.

A deepwater port was opened in 1963, access being via a 43-mile (70km) channel to Suisun Bay which enabled fruit, vegetables, grains, sugar beets, and dairy goods from the fertile Sacramento Valley to be exported. The waterfront enjoyed a resurgence with a public market, new public docks, excursion cruises, a water taxi, a waterfront hotel, and two new restaurants.

Old Sacramento, which attracts over five million visitors annually, is home of one of the largest jazz festivals in the world.

Points of interest include the state capitol in its beautiful park setting; the former governor's mansion, a museum since 1968; Sutter's Fort; the Crocker Art Museum; and the Golden State Museum. The city's trademark flower is the camellia, and a festival is held annually along with the California State Fair and Exposition.

RIGHT: *At right, the 1201K Tower—the "Roll-on" building—designed by Hellmuth, Obata & Kassabaum, the largest architectural firm in the world, and built in 1992. In the center of the photograph is the Baroque Cathedral of the Blessed Sacrament. Built in 1886, it was inspired by the Church of the Holy Trinity in Paris. The tallest building in the city is the 380ft US Bank Plaza built in 1991 designed to look like the great Art Deco skyscrapers of the 1920s.*
© Buddy Mays/CORBIS

ABOVE: *Locomotive at Sacramento Rail Fair—the California State Railroad Museum is based in the city.* © Morton Beebe/CORBIS

OVERLEAF: *The neoclassical California State Capitol was built in 1884 and reaches 247ft in height.* © Bruce Burkhardt/CORBIS

OVERLEAF, INSET: *Sacramento's Tower Bridge.* © Gerald French/CORBIS

SALT LAKE CITY

Location 40.760°N 111.89°W
Area 109.1 square miles
Altitude 4,266 feet above sea level
City Population 181,743
Time Zone Mountain Daylight Saving

Salt Lake City, nearly 4,300 feet (1,300 metres) above sea level, came into being in 1847, when a group of around 150 Mormon pioneers led by Brigham Young became the first non-Indians to settle in the valley. They named the settlement after a salty inland lake which dominated the desert to the west. More emigrants arrived, many European converts to the religion. They gave Salt Lake City a cosmopolitan character. Mexico ceded the region to the United States in 1848, and in 1850, the "State of Desert" became the Utah Territory. In 1896, Utah finally became the 45th state.

Utah was connected to the east and west coasts in 1869 when the first transcontinental railroad was built by city founder Young. Many copper, silver, gold, and lead mines were opened, while mine owners built opulent villas on Brigham Street.

The 1890s and early 1900s brought many changes as the State Capitol and other historic buildings were built and a streetcar-based transport system assembled. City parks were built, sewer systems and street lighting were installed, and streets were paved. Between 1900 and 1930, the city's population nearly tripled. The Depression brought construction to a standstill, but World War II saw military installations revitalize the economy.

During the 1960s several commercial and service centers were built in the suburbs, drawing business away from downtown. To help counteract this movement, the Mormon Church invested $40 million in development of a city-center shopping mall. Salt Lake continued to grow in the 1990s as the population exceeded 160,000, when the Salt Palace Convention Center was rebuilt and a major office tower and new courts complex were constructed. The Salt Lake City International Airport added a new runway.

The success of the 2002 Olympic Winter Games brought growth in Salt Lake's hotel industry, while transport projects included TRAX, a $312 million light-rail system. Monuments to their founder include Brigham Young's home (known as the Beehive House) and the Brigham Young Monument (1897).

OVERLEAF: *Salt Lake City below the Wasatch Range. Part of the Rocky Mountains that extend c.250 miles south from southeast Idaho to central Utah, the highest peak of the range is Mount Timpanogos (12,008ft).* © Joseph Sohm; Visions of America/CORBIS

LEFT: *Salt Lake City at dusk: the State Capitol sits on a hill overlooking the city and has done so since 1915—it is said that it overlooked the Salt Lake Temple to symbolize the fact that the state was a higher authority than the church. Today the 1972 LDS Office Building (center of photograph, 420ft)—the main office building for the Church of Jesus Christ of Latter-day Saints (Mormons)—in Temple Square has reversed the position.* © Mark E. Gibson/CORBIS

ABOVE: *The tallest building (422ft) in Salt Lake City is the Wells Fargo Center also known as the American Stores Center which was built in 1998. The top of the roof is 4,691ft above sea level.* © Richard Cummins/CORBIS

DELTA CENTER

SAN ANTONIO

Location 29.423°N 98.493°W
Area 407.6 square miles
Altitude 512 feet above sea level
City Population 1,144,646
Time Zone Central

The eighth largest city in the United States, San Antonio has always been a meeting place for many cultures. Spanish explorers, who came upon a native American Indian settlement by what is now the San Antonio River in 1691, named it after the feast day of St. Anthony. Father Antonio Olivares founded Mission San Antonio de Valero in 1718, and in 1836 this entered the history books as the Alamo after 189 defending troops held out against a 4,000-strong Mexican army for 13 days. The Alamo is now a shrine and museum.

During the 1810–21 Mexican Revolution, common interests in securing freedom from Spain saw Americans fighting alongside Mexicans in several key battles. At the war's end, although Texas became a Mexican state, 3,500 American settlers quickly moved into the area.

The city's subsequent growth was largely due to a strong military presence: Fort Sam Houston, where army legends like Pershing, Stilwell, Krueger, and Eisenhower all served, was joined by Kelly Air Force Base in 1917, these being followed by Lackland, Randolph, and Brooks Air Force bases. Fort Sam is headquarters for the Fifth U.S. Army and the Health Services Command, and the military is still the city's third biggest source of employment after tourism and medicine/biotechnology.

In 1921, floods destroyed Downtown San Antonio, drowning as many as 50 people. As a result, the Olmos Dam was constructed to handle the overflow. Outstanding current buildings include Rivercenter shopping and entertainment complex and the Henry B. Gonzalez Convention Center.

San Antonio has two major theme parks—Sea World San Antonio, the world's largest marine life park, and Six Flags Fiesta Texas. The San Antonio Museum of Art (SAMA) is housed in the former headquarters of the Lone Star Brewery while the opulent Majestic Theater, built in 1929, stages touring Broadway shows and is home to the San Antonio Symphony Orchestra.

RIGHT: *Aerial view of San Antonio and the San Antonio River.* © Richard Cummins/CORBIS

FAR RIGHT: *The tallest structure in San Antonio is an observation tower—the Tower of the Americas (622ft) built in 1968 for the Hemisfair World's Fair that celebrated San Antonio's 250th anniversary. This is the neo-Gothic Tower Life Building built in 1929.* © D. Boone/CORBIS

OVERLEAF: *The Alamo at night.* © Joseph Sohm; Visions of America/CORBIS

CROCKETT
HOTEL

SAN DIEGO

Location 32.71°N 117.156°W
Area 324.3 square miles
Altitude 40 feet above sea level
City Population 1,223,400
Time Zone Pacific Daylight Saving

San Diego was originally founded by the Portuguese explorer Juan Rodriguez Cabrillo when he landed in what is now San Diego Bay and claimed the area for Spain on September 28, 1542. Cabrillo named the port San Miguel, in honor of St. Michael the Archangel whose feast day was on the following day.

The settlement, the first European settlement in California, remained San Miguel until Sebastian Vizcaino sailed into the bay on November 10, 1602, and renamed it San Diego for San Diego de Alcala (St. Didicus). It became a city in 1769.

Due to its magnificent location beside the Pacific Ocean, San Diego quickly became an important center for the U.S. Navy. With its great weather, miles of sandy beaches, and many major attractions, it has also become known as one of the best tourist destinations anywhere in the world. The city also sits beside the international border with Mexico and 20 miles north of Tijuana.

The city contains the major theme parks like Legoland, SeaWorld, and Balboa Park which contains an art gallery, several museums (including an aerospace museum), and the world-famous San Diego Zoo and Wild Animal Park. As for culture, San Diego has two Tony Award-winning theaters, over 90 museums and stages festivals showcasing the city's ethnic diversity. Some buildings remain from the Panama-California International Exposition (1915-16) and the California Pacific International Exposition (1935-36), while Horton Plaza, a huge shopping mall that won awards for its dramatic architecture, was the jewel in the crown of a 1980s urban revitalization program.

As well as being an important naval port, San Diego has become a nationally recognized center for wireless industries telecommunications, biotechnology, software, and electronics, the city being dubbed Telecom Valley. It is currently the second largest city in California and the seventh largest in the United States.

RIGHT: *Coronado Island Ferry Dock with the city in the distance.* © Richard Cummins/CORBIS

OVERLEAF: *San Diego waterfront at sunset. At far right San Diego's tallest building—One America Plaza (500ft) built in 1991 with KMA the executive architect and Helmut Jahn the design architect.* © Joseph Sohm; ChromoSohm Inc./CORBIS

Left: *Beachgoers enjoy the July weather at Pacific Beach in San Diego, CA. Thousands of people head to the beaches and parks in anticipation of 4th of July festivities.* © Getty Images

John Burnham & Co.
BEST WESTERN BAYSIDE INN

PAC

SAN FRANCISCO

Location 37.775°N 122.418°W
Area 46.7 square miles
Altitude 63 feet above sea level
City Population 776,733
Time Zone Pacific Daylight Saving

San Francisco—renowned for its beautiful setting being bordered by the Pacific Ocean, the Golden Gate strait and San Bruno Mountain—is mainly sited on the northern tip of a peninsula at the entrance to San Francisco Bay. The city is completed by a group of islands, namely the famous Alcatraz, Angel, Farallon, Treasure, and Yerba Buena. It is a leading financial and international trade center for the western United States.

The city's roots were established in 1776 when Spanish officer Juan Bautista de Anza built a fort to protect the entrance to the bay, while at the same time Father Junípero Serra built the nearby Misión San Francisco de Asís. Little development occurred until a third settlement was established at Yerba Buena Cove (near the present site of Portsmouth Square) and this was claimed from Mexico by the United States in 1846, who renamed it San Francisco a year later.

Gold was discovered near Sacramento in 1848 and the well documented gold rush transformed San Francisco into a booming community, the city being incorporated two years later. It also developed as a port and an early government center, renowned for its cosmopolitan feel and lawlessness, particularly in the Barbary Coast area, while the railroad reached the city in 1869.

In 1906 a devastating earthquake caused a fire that raged for three days, destroying almost all of the downtown and residential areas. San Francisco was quickly rebuilt but experts regularly predict another huge shift in the San Andreas Fault; the last to date occurred in 1989.

During World War II, the city was a major shipbuilding center and, at the end of the hostilities, an international conference was held that drafted the charter of the United Nations.

The city, home to the Giants baseball team and the 49ers football team, has been a center for gay rights activism since the 1970s. The AIDS Memorial Grove was designated a national landmark in 1996 and the 15 acres of parkland that surround it are a beautiful tribute to those it remembers.

RIGHT: *The San Francisco skyline is dominated by the futuristic Transamerica Pyramid (853ft) built in 1972. Transamerica wanted a taller building (1,150ft) but the city would not approve it because it interfered with views of the Bay from Nob Hill.* © Gerald French/CORBIS

FAR RIGHT: *Victorian Homes, Alamo Square, and San Francisco skyline.* © Charles O'Rear/CORBIS

PORT OF
SAN FRANCISCO

San Francisco skyline, Transamerica Pyramid at right; the city's second tallest building, the 1969-built Bank of America Center (779ft), is to its left. © Charles O'Rear/CORBIS

SAN JOSÉ

Location 37.339°N 121.893°W
Area 174.9 square miles
Altitude 87 feet above sea level
City Population 924,950
Time Zone Pacific Daylight Saving

Burt Bacharach and Hal David's song *Do You Know The Way To San José* put the name of northern California's largest city in the pop spotlight in 1968. Since then it has become the capital of Silicon Valley, the high-tech manufacturing area, and, at 175 square miles, contains more than two-thirds of the Valley's total population. It considers itself the gateway to the Bay Area.

Situated on the banks of the Guadalupe River, San José was founded in 1777 as the first civil settlement in Spanish California and was named El Pueblo de San José de Guadalupe after the husband of the Virgin Mary. Its first function was to supply provisions to the nearby military forts on Monterey to the south and San Francisco to the north.

Things moved slowly until 1846 when California became part of the United States. A goldrush two years later brought many settlers to the area, and the population passed 3,000 in 1850. Unfortunately, San José's infrastructure didn't cope particularly well and it had its status as the state capital removed in 1851.

The latter half of the century saw agriculture hold sway, with fruit processing plants and canneries built (San José and the Santa Clara Valley has the oldest continuously producing vineyards in California), but the pendulum swung in the 20th century towards manufacturing industry. As aerospace and electronics grew, the area of the city multiplied tenfold in the three postwar decades from 1950. But cuts in defence spending after the collapse of the cold war caused problems.

San José, with a population little short of million, is the third largest city in California and the 11th largest in the nation. A new city hall with a water feature was under construction in 2004.

RIGHT: *In 1884, wealthy widow Sarah L. Winchester's house was started: 38 years later the Winchester Rifle heiress died, the house still unfinished. The 160 rooms are filled with state-of-the-art Victorian technology—gas lights that operated by pressing a button, three elevators, and 47 fireplaces—and beautiful details: parquet floors, gold and silver chandeliers, and Tiffany art-glass windows.* © Robert Holmes/CORBIS

FAR RIGHT: *Silicon Valley—the San Francisco Bay Area High Tech Area has revolutionized the world and San José experienced a boom due to the large number of high-tech companies in the region.* © Gerald French/CORBIS

OVERLEAF, LEFT: *San José Mission.* © Bo Zaunders/CORBIS

OVERLEAF, RIGHT: *The Tech Museum of Innovation adds a colorful dimension to San José's architecture.* © David McNew/Newsmakers

SILICON VALLEY

SEATTLE

Location 47.606°N 122.33°W
Area 83.9 square miles
Altitude 350 feet above sea level
City Population 563,374
Time Zone Pacific Daylight Saving

Famous in modern times as being the home of the Jumbo Jet and then Microsoft, Seattle's early prosperity depended on timber and gold. Its name comes from a local Indian Chief Sealth who befriended the first settlers when they arrived in 1851–52.

The city's location between the Cascade and Olympic mountain ranges made it a natural gateway to the forests of the northwest; many millions of logs were processed by steam-powered lumber mills, loaded onto steamships, and transported worldwide. The goldrush in Alaska in 1897 also played a part in building the city. A railroad link was completed in 1893, the Great Northern Railway turning a small lumber town into a transportation hub. Four years earlier, the so-called Great Fire had razed 25 blocks in the centre of Seattle to the ground. This enabled drainage and sewage problems to be solved during rebuilding.

William Boeing arrived in 1916, initially to launch an air-mail service to Canada. He stayed to found Boeing Aviation which, along with Microsoft, founded by Seattle native Bill Gates, has run the local economy ever since. Chemicals, machinery, textiles, and clothing are among other products synonymous with Seattle.

Seattle's 600-foot (183m) Space Needle was built in 1962 for the Century 21 World's Fair and remains a land-mark today, while the Tech Museum of Innovation and the city's repertory theater both acquired striking new buildings in 1998.

The city's impressive parks include Alum Rock Park, with its mineral springs; Kelley Park, with a zoo and a Japanese garden; and Rosicrucian Park, with an Egyptian museum and a planetarium. in 1982, Seattle was ranked as the number one recreational city in America.

In 2001 an earthquake damaged the city, mainly in the Pioneer Square area, but caused few casualties among its 500,000-plus inhabitants.

RIGHT: *Skyline of Seattle, Washington. At far right the Bank of America Tower (937ft) built in 1985, whose rooftop is 1,042.5ft above sea level. At left, the second-tallest building—the Washington Mutual Tower (772ft).* © Lester Lefkowitz/CORBIS

FAR RIGHT: *Pioneer Square pergola.* © Randy Faris/CORBIS

ZASU
PIONEER

FAR LEFT: *Seattle skyline with Mount Rainier backdrop. At right, the 1961 Space Needle, originally called the Space Cage and its restaurant the Eye of the Needle. It is 605ft tall, the brainchild of Edward E. Carlson (1911–90), a Seattle civic leader and former CEO of United Airlines, and the centerpiece of the 1962 Century 21 Exposition.*
© Ken Straiton/CORBIS

LEFT: *Walrus head sculpture on the facade of the Arctic Club Building.*
© Paul A. Souders/CORBIS

ST. LOUIS

Location 44.948°N 93.347°W
Area 61.9 square miles
Altitude 465 feet above sea level
City Population 44,126
Time Zone Central

Built on the banks of the Mississippi River, St. Louis was French and Spanish before it was American. Before that, an Indian civilization built the huge, mysterious earthen structures that gave St. Louis its earliest nickname, "Mound City."

In 1764, French fur traders from New Orleans named their settlement for King Louis IX (1214–70). The joining of the Mississippi and Missouri rivers was the ideal site from which to trade with Native Americans. France regained rights to St. Louis in 1800, but Napoleon sold Louisiana to President Thomas Jefferson in 1803 without taking possession, at a stroke doubling the size of the United States.

The steamboat era arrived in 1817, turning the Mississippi River into a formidable trade route. One-third of the city went up in flames, however, when the steamboat *White Cloud* exploded on the riverfront. Two historic structures—the Old Courthouse and Old Cathedral, both of which survive today—were saved. The arrival of the railway in 1874, saw steamboat traffic decline; Union Station, once the country's largest railroad terminal, now houses shops and a hotel.

St. Louis became a major industrial center with more than 100 breweries operating in the city. The largest, Anheuser-Busch, has its headquarters in the city. A World's Fair, the Louisiana Purchase Exposition in 1904, drew 20 million visitors while the Olympic Games took place that same year. Charles Lindbergh named the plane that took him from New York to Paris in 1927 in an historic solo flight the *Spirit of St. Louis*, spreading its fame still further.

Landmarks of the city include the 630ft (192m) high Gateway Arch, unveiled in 1965 as a tribute to Jefferson's vision of a continental United States, the Museum of Westward Expansion and the Old Courthouse; the three comprise the Jefferson National Expansion Memorial. Others to be commemorated include explorers Lewis and Clark and ragtime composer Scott Joplin. There are also two museums of contemporary art, the Pulitzer Foundation for the Arts and the Contemporary Art Museum.

RIGHT: *The St. Louis skyline and Gateway Arch, created by Eero Saarinen and Associates, the nation's tallest memorial. The Museum of Westward Expansion is underground below the arch.* © Owaki-Kulla/CORBIS

FAR RIGHT: *Downtown St. Louis in the evening.* © Conrad Zobel/CORBIS

JEFFERSON BANK
100

FAR LEFT: *The Old Courthouse is part of the Jefferson National Expansion Monument; Architect William Rumbold modeled the wrought and cast iron dome after St. Peter's Basilica in Rome.* © Richard Hamilton Smith/CORBIS

St. Louis Art Museum. © Jan Butchofsky-Houser/CORBIS

TAMPA

Location 27.947°N 82.458°W
Area 112.1 square miles
Altitude 48 feet above sea level
City Population 303,447
Time Zone Eastern Daylight Saving

Situated on the idyllic Gulf Coast and with a population of just over 300,000, the city of Tampa has attracted many of its inhabitants through the holiday market—vacationers who didn't want to go home. They followed in the footsteps of the Spanish conquistadores under explorer Ponce de Leon who took over from the native American Indians. Further cosmopolitan influences came from two groups of fishermen, the Cubans and the Greeks, the latter specializing in diving for sponge. Cuban cigar-making also became a local industry, the Ybor City area also being the center of Tampa's Hispanic population.

In 1824, four companies of the U.S. Army established Fort Brooke to protect the strategic harbor at Tampa Bay. The territory became part of the United States in 1845.

The arrival of the railway in 1884 brought prosperity and resulted in the building of several hotels, the most famous being the minaret-topped Tampa Bay Hotel which was modeled on a Spanish castle. This now houses the Henry B. Plant museum, appropriately named after the railway mogul who connected Tampa with the rest of the United States.

When phosphates were discovered in the late 1880s, the resulting mining and shipping industries prompted a boom, and Tampa's port is now the seventh largest in the nation and a major point of entry to the Sunshine State for the holiday trade. Tampa has evolved into a multicultural, diverse business center, the downtown business district having grown phenomenally since the 1960s. Major banks and an increasing number of other corporations occupy large glass, steel, and concrete buildings that tower high above the bay. The Tampa Convention Center, overlooking the Hillsborough River, offers meeting facilities and features an "erupting" fire and water sculpture.

Tampa's suburbs were consolidated with the city In 1953, almost doubling its population, and three long bridges link Tampa with Clearwater and St. Petersburg, on the Pinellas peninsula. Tourist attractions include the Busch Gardens zoo and theme park.

RIGHT: *Tampa skyline and Hillsborough River.* © Richard Cummins/CORBIS

FAR RIGHT: *The Sunshine Skyway Bridge stands 183ft above Tampa Bay spanning 4.1 miles of I-275.* © Raymond Gehman/CORBIS

A spiraling yellow roller coaster gives riders a thrill at Busch Gardens amusement and wildlife park in Tampa, Florida. © Nik Wheeler/CORBIS

FAR RIGHT: *The Siboney Building, an example of Spanish style in Ybor City, a former Cuban enclave in Tampa. The building features clay tile roof and brightly colored painted tile around the doorways and windows. It was built c. 1988.* © William A. Bake/CORBIS

15 MINUTE
LOAD &
UNLOAD
ONLY

TUCSON

Location 32.221°N 110.925°W
Area 194.7 square miles
Altitude 2483 feet above sea level
City Population 486,699
Time Zone Mountain Standard

One of America's most multicultural cities, Tucson's traditions span centuries of habitation from prehistoric Indian cultures through Spanish, Mexican, and Native American influences to recent immigrants from Malaysia. It is believed to be the oldest continually inhabited city in the United States, its prehistoric roots dating back 15,000 years.

In 1692, Spanish missionaries arrived in the valley to find an Indian village named S-tukson or "black base" on the bank of the Santa Cruz River. In 1775, the Spanish built an outpost, the Presidio of San Augustin; this is the official birthdate of the City of Tucson. The arrival of a Spanish Jesuit priest, Father Francisco Kino, in 1694 had a major impact on the development of southern Arizona. He established a chain of missions from Mexico to the Pacific Ocean, and introduced European plants and livestock. Eventually, Spanish oppression prompted years of struggle and violence as the Indians rebelled.

Tucson became part of Mexico when that country fought for independence from Spain in 1821, but fell under the jurisdiction of the United States in 1854 when the U.S. negotiated the Gadsden Purchase. After a brief period under the Confederate flag during the civil war, Tucson was chosen as the capitol of the new U.S. territory of Arizona. As western settlers continued to arrive, Tucson gained a reputation as a rough frontier town.

In 1880, the Southern Pacific Railroad reached the territorial capital with a population of 8,000. Around the turn of the century, Tucson began attracting thousands of tuberculosis victims seeking a cure in its dry climate. Arizona became the 48th state of the Union in 1912.

During World War II, Davis-Monthan Field became an important U.S. Air Force training base. Many airmen subsequently returned to Tucson to settle or retire. Fueled by postwar industries and tourism, the population grew rapidly —at one point welcoming 1,000 newcomers each month.

By 1950 Tucson's population has reached 120,000 and nearly doubled to 220,000 in the following decade. By 1990, as its population topped 400,000, it was the 33rd largest U.S. city, while the population doubled yet again in the following decade.

RIGHT: *Saguaro cacti in the desert near Tucson.* Carnegiea gigantea *can be found through the Sonoran Desert of extreme southeastern California, southern Arizona, and adjoining northwestern Mexico. The state flower of Arizona, the Saguaro has a tall, fluted, spiny stem at between 18 and 24 inches in diameter, often with several large branches curving upward. When water is absorbed, the outer pulp of the Saguaro expands. Creamy-white, three-inch-wide flowers with yellow centers bloom in May and June. Clustered near the ends of branches, the blossoms open during cooler desert nights and close again by next midday.* © D. Boone/CORBIS

ABOVE: *St. Augustine Cathedral is reflected in skyscraper glass. The original plans for the church were for a Gothic structure with pointed spires. Lack of funds stopped this and 30 years later Bishop Daniel Gercke, the first U.S.-born bishop of Tucson, started the work we see today, including the magnificent cast stone facade—inspired by the Cathedral of Querétaro, Mexico—completed in 1928. With the exception of the facade and towers, the cathedral was demolished and rebuilt in the late 1960s under the leadership of Bishop Francis J. Green.* © Danny Lehman/CORBIS

RIGHT: *The Tucson skyline. The tallest structure (at right) is the UniSource Energy Tower, also known as Wells Fargo Tower, which is 330ft tall and was completed in 1986. To its left is the Bank of America Plaza (262ft) completed in 1977.* © Danny Lehman/CORBIS

TULSA

Location 36.153°N 95.992°W
Area 182.6 square miles
Altitude 740 feet above sea level
City Population 393,049
Time Zone Central

The Native American settlement known as Tallahassee founded in 1836 on the east side of the Arkansas River is the genesis of modern-day Tulsa. The Cherokees, Choctaws, Chickasaws, Creeks, and Seminoles—forced out of their homelands into Indian Territory—brought with them the concepts of trading and commerce that would shape both the city and the state of Oklahoma. In 1846, Lewis Perryman built a log cabin trading post near what is now 33rd Street and South Rockford Avenue.

The Civil War forced many to flee the area. But the arrival of the railroad in 1882, when the St. Louis and San Francisco Railroad extended its line to serve the cattle business, the city's first industry, and the establishment of the Post Office in March 1879 saw the name Tulsa adopted; by the time the city was incorporated in 1898, the population had grown to 1,100.

The discovery of oil at Red Fork, across the river from Tulsa, brought an influx of people. Many brought their families to one of the few safe frontier cities. In 1905, the Glenn Pool oil field laid the foundation for Tulsa to become a leader in many businesses related to oil and gas, in addition to being the physical center of the growing petroleum industry.

An airport was an early addition to the city, and the aerospace industry followed as American Airlines built a major maintenance center and the SABRE reservation system relocated from New York. There are now more than 300 aviation-related companies in Tulsa. Many international corporations have made Tulsa their home including American Airlines, Kimberly-Clark, Ford Glass, and Avis.

In the 1920s, the Arkansas River was replaced as a water source by water from the Spavinaw Hills. This was considered to be one of the largest public works projects in the country during this era when citizens of Tulsa supported a multi-million dollar bond. In 1970 the Port of Catoosa linked Tulsa with the rest of the world via river navigation to the Mississippi River and the Gulf of Mexico.

Redevelopment of the city began in the early 1950s. The growth of Tulsa to the south led to the construction of the 51st Street Bridge, dedicated in 1953. The 1960s saw early downtown commercial buildings make way for modern high-rises. By 1980, Tulsa's population stood at 360,919, ranking it the 38th largest city in the nation. Vestiges of its Native American heritage and oil boom days are still visible.

RIGHT: *Tulsa at night. At right the twin towers of the Holy Family Cathedral, built in 1919.* © Annie Griffiths Belt/CORBIS

LEFT: *110 West 7th Building (388ft) is the backdrop to Boston Avenue Methodist Church completed in 1929.*
© Annie Griffiths Belt/CORBIS

LEFT: *View of Downtown Tulsa from above the Sun Refinery. At left One Williams Center (667ft) built 1976, the tallest building in Oklahoma; to its right the ornate 320 South Boston Building. The original 10-story building was completed in 1917 and expanded to 400ft in 1929. In the foreground, the Red Fork Expressway carries I-244 over the Arkansas River. Alongside, but not visible, is the historic 11th Street Bridge over which Route 66 ran toward Oklahoma City. Built in 1915 for just $180,000, the bridge has been unused since 1972 when I-244 bypassed it. It has recently been named after Cyrus Avery, who is known as the Father of Route 66 and was instrumental in its routing and naming.* © Annie Griffiths Belt/CORBIS

VIRGINIA BEACH

Location 36.852°N 75.978°W
Area 248.3 square miles
Altitude 15 feet above sea level
City Population 425,257
Time Zone Eastern Daylight Saving

The history of Virginia Beach dates back to 1607, when three vessels stopped at the mouth of the Chesapeake Bay, naming the location Cape Henry before sailing upriver and settling the first permanent English colony in the New World at Jamestown. (A granite cross at Cape Henry now marks the spot.) The population of surrounding Princess Anne County grew apace, and trade flourished to such an extent that bonfires were used to guide vessels safely through the Bay before the Cape Henry Lighthouse was built in 1792. Virginia Beach also became a popular holiday destination after railroad services began in 1883.

The Oceana Naval Air Station, established in World War II, is one of four major military installations in Virginia Beach—Little Creek (a naval amphibious training center), Fort Story (U.S. Army Transportation Command), and Dam Neck (the U.S. fleet anti-air warfare training center) the others—put the city on the strategic map.

The merger of Princess Anne County and the town of Virginia Beach in 1963 created the largest city in Virginia which claims to be the largest resort city in the world. It begins at the North Carolina state line, extends north for 28 miles along the Atlantic coast to the mouth of the Chesapeake Bay and thence to Norfolk. The Chesapeake Bay Bridge–Tunnel (opened 1964) links Virginia Beach with the eastern shore of Virginia and Maryland.

The City of Virginia Beach has enjoyed a steady rate of growth in population as well as visitors. It currently hosts the East Coast Surfing Championship, while deep sea fishing trips are among many other water-related pastimes on offer. Visitor attractions include the previously mentioned Cape Henry lighthouse from the late 18th century, the nation's oldest brick residence which dates from 1636, and the Alan B. Shepard civic center, named after the astronaut.

RIGHT: *A crowed beach filled with visitors, swimmers, and sunbathers enjoy the fine weather on the Memorial Day weekend.* © Jim Sugar/CORBIS

RIGHT INSET: *The oldest government-built lighthouse in America, dating back to 1791, and the traditional symbol of Virginia Beach, the Cape Henry Lighthouse—the tallest cast-iron lighthouse in the country—has been guiding ships safely into the Chesapeake Bay since 1881.* © Richard T. Nowitz/CORBIS

FAR RIGHT: *The regular lines of a housing community in suburban Virginia Beach.* © John Henley/CORBIS

VERGENNES

Location 44.167°N 73.254°W
Area 2.4 square miles
Altitude 205 feet above sea level
City Population 2,741
Time Zone Eastern Daylight Saving

Named after Count Vergennes, the French foreign minister who supported the colonies during the Revolution, the compact city of Vergennes is located in the northwest quadrant of Addison County. Vermont decided to create its first city on the site of the Otter Creek Falls, an ideal site for industry to develop, in 1788 when the nearby towns of Panton, Ferrisburgh, and New Haven declined to fund a new industrial center outside their boundaries. Early industries included iron, local forges producing ammunition for American troops during the war of 1812.

The start of the 19th century saw Vergennes take significant steps forward, even though a bid to become state capital was unsuccessful. A group of Boston merchants formed the Monkton Iron Company to take advantage of President Jefferson's embargo. When the country went to war with Britain, Commodore Thomas MacDonough chose Vergennes as his naval base, but his victory at Plattsburgh Bay and the subsequent end of the war closed this eventful period of the city's history.

Manufacturers, merchants and professional men, rather than farmers, comprised the bulk of the city's early population. Vergennes became Vermont's largest shipping port after the opening of the Champlain Canal in 1823, and would continue to grow with the coming of the railroad. A flow of lumber from Canada led to wood-finishing companies arising until new tariffs in the 1890s ended this duty-free trade.

Vergennes remained a regional, industrial, and commercial center into the 20th century. The Vermont Shade Roller Company was joined as a major employer by a hydro-electric plant and the L.F. Benton spark-plug factory. But the biggest, Simmonds Precision Products, went through a downsizing in the 1990s, emphasizing the risks of relying on one employer. The city is now attempting to attract other companies to broaden its industrial base.

Recreational attractions include Button Bay State Park, and D.A.R. State Park, while Lake Champlain Maritime Museum is a major site of historic interest.

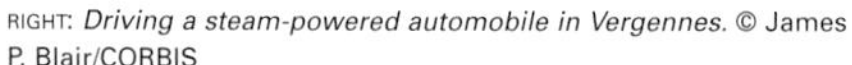

RIGHT: *Driving a steam-powered automobile in Vergennes.* © James P. Blair/CORBIS

FAR RIGHT: *Otter Creek Falls flows into Lake Champlain along Vergennes, Vermont.* © James P. Blair/CORBIS

WASHINGTON

Location 38.9°N 77.016°W
Area 61.4 square miles
Altitude 9 feet above sea level
City Population 572,059
Time Zone Eastern Daylight Saving

Washington and its surrounding district was established as a federal territory in 1790 as the site of the new nation's permanent capital. Named after the first U.S. President, George Washington, it has been the seat of federal government since 1800. The District of Columbia takes its name from the explorer who found America, Christopher Columbus.

Washington has always struggled to maintain a balance between being a city in its own right and its role as capital of the United States. George Washington, however, disagreed with this view and believed that the capital was fundamental in building the nation. Eminent French architect Pierre l'Enfant was hired to build the city and laid out the central town in 1791, but was so entangled in disputes that he was fired a year later. The federal district was, therefore, far from the finished article by the time the national government arrived in 1800.

After the Civil War ended in 1865, Republicans within Congress seized the chance to implement social reforms in Washington. It was, therefore, the first city to enforce the emancipation of slaves and end segregation on public transport. All references to race were eliminated from the civil code and black males were granted voting rights. In 1871, the cities of Washington and Georgetown were consolidated with Washington County to become Washington D.C., thereby making the city, county, and federal district one.

Several generations of reformers wanted to secure better housing conditions and in the 1930s Washington formed the nation's first public housing authority. The city has retained some aspects of its southern origin, but has assumed a much more cosmopolitan character.

Washington is home to many famous public buildings and monuments many of which are associated with federal government. The city includes the J. Edgar Hoover Building, the headquarters of the FBI and, of course, the White House, official residence of the U.S. President.

RIGHT AND OVERLEAF: *Views of the Mall and the Lincoln Memorial, the 555ft Washington Memorial and the U.S. Capitol.* © Larry Lee Photography/CORBIS

FAR RIGHT: *Union Station was designed by D. H. Burnham and completed in 1907. The main waiting room (seen here) was designed after the great hall in the baths of Diocletian.* © Bettmann/CORBIS

ATES 16 & 17

WICHITA

Location 37.692°N 97.337°W
Area 135.8 square miles
Altitude 1,305 feet above sea level
City Population 344,284
Time Zone Central

The largest city in Kansas and the county seat of Sedgwick County, Wichita was built on a site that had served as a trading center for at least 11,000 years. The area was first visited by Coronado in the 16th century, who encountered a tribe of Indians he called Quiviras but which were later identified, following archaeological and historical studies, as Wichita Indians. This tribe moved south to Oklahoma by 1719 and traded with French settlers but returned to the area in 1863 due to their pro-Union tendencies during the Civil War. They then became the first settlers in the area, building a collection of grass houses. In 1870 the city became officially incorporated, later to become a railhead destination for the cattle drives from Texas, thus earning its first nickname of "Cowtown."

The discovery of oil nearby following drilling in 1914 brought considerable investment into the city and led to the creation of an airplane industry during the 1920s with 43 Swallow planes, the first type made specifically for production, being built in three years. By the end of World War II, production in Wichita had increased and more than four bombers a day were rolling off the production lines. One-time employees of Swallow included Lloyd Stearman, who later formed Stearman Aircraft (a predecessor of Boeing), Walter Beech, who formed Beech Aircraft, and Clyde Cessna, who formed Cessna Aircraft. Other major airplane companies in the city include LearJet and Airbus Industrie, hence its current nickname of Air Capital. Other industries and businesses that started in Wichita include Pizza Hut, Koch Industries, and Coleman. The city is also an important education center within the state, and has two universities, including Wichita State University. A population of 279,000 in 1980 had grown to nearly 350,000 two decades later.

Wichita's other claim to fame came in 1900 when the Women's Christian Temperance Union focused their attention on the city and tried to close down the city's drinking establishments. Led by WCTU member Carrie Nation, the Carey House bar was smashed up by rocks and a pool ball!

RIGHT: *Lightning over Downtown Wichita.* © Jim Reed/CORBIS

FAR RIGHT: *More bad weather—drivers navigate through heavy snow and white out conditions during a Wichita snowstorm. It's not just in* The Wizard of Oz *that Kansas endures bad weather; tornadoes are a frequent visitors to the plains.* © Jim Reed/CORBIS

OVERLEAF: *Frost on trees in Wichita.* © Jim Reed/CORBIS